A
Trip
To Freedom

A Trip To Freedom

How I used God's Word to end abuse in all
relationships and be totally set free of the damage
from forty-five years of severe abuse.

Ruth Johnson

Lighthouse of Hope Publications
Mill Creek, Washington, U.S.A.

A TRIP TO FREEDOM
Second Edition – September 2005
First Edition – January 1998
ISBN 978-0-9661470-5-6
Library of Congress Catalog Card Number: 2005906794
Copyright © 2005 Lighthouse of Hope Publications

Published by:
Lighthouse of Hope Publications
PMB #365
914 164th Street S.E. #B-12
Mill Creek, Washington, U.S.A. 98012-6339

iv

Dedication

I dedicate this book to all the hurting men and women who have found little or no lasting solution to their pain.

I also dedicate it to my children, Mary, John and Paul. I love them more than they can ever know and I'm so proud of the special people they have each become.

Acknowledgments

I extend the heartfelt gratitude of my husband, Barry and I to Alice Hay. We deeply cherish her encouragement of what the Father has called us to bring to the Body of Christ.

> *"Thank you, Alice, for being a treasure to the heart of the Father and a beloved woman of God to us. You have deeply touched us with your kindness and love. Never can we thank the Father enough for bringing you into our lives and encouraging us through your love."*

I also extend our undying gratitude to Nick and Sheila Stark. Barry and I profoundly appreciate the impact this couple had on the birth of *"A Trip To Freedom"* many years ago.

> *"Thank you, Nick and Sheila, for being the catalyst that the Father used to initially make this very special book a published reality. May He bless you all the days of your lives because of the generations upon generations of miracles that were made possible because you believed in how much the Father could use 'A Trip To Freedom' to set people free."*

A very personal message from the author...

I was forty-five years old before I stopped hurting and my life-long pattern of choosing destructive relationships was finally over. How I wish that anyone reading *"A Trip To Freedom"* would not have wait as long as I did to experience this breakthrough.

In this book are the keys that opened the door for me into that amazing transformation. It was written after I carefully recorded for fourteen years every revelation God gave me into how to end my tormenting emotional pain.

If you are searching for a way to resolve the hurts from your past and to stop the discouraging treadmill of choosing destructive relationships, this personal message is for you...

While I wrote "A Trip To Freedom," my passion was that in its pages you would discover the truths that will unlock a lasting closure to the pain from your past. Through the years I have seen the Father give this miracle to countless people who had despaired of ever being able to stop hurting. He wants to give this same healing gift to you.

As you read this book, I will bare my soul to you in very honest ways.

I'm going to be this transparent so that what I have learned about being radically set free from forty-five years of severe abuse can be passed on to you as a priceless inheritance.

In the pages of this book, there are also treasures from the Word that will help you know how the Father really does feel about you.

So at different moments, as you read "A Trip To Freedom," I strongly encourage you to pause and talk to the Father. I encourage you to tell Him all about your desperate desire for His help and let Him know exactly how you are feeling.

If tears come, my wish for you is that you will let them spill out of your heart to Him. During those moments of vulnerability, the Father longs and even aches to gently lead you out of the tormenting valley of your pain to a place of safety and healing.

Each time I was this real with the Father, He didn't disappoint me. As I opened up the depths of my soul to Him, He became my very real Dad and I have never been the same. In His compassionate Father's love I finally found the miracle of healing for my troubled soul that I had searched for all of my life.

If you pour out your heart to the Father, He won't disappoint you as well. He will meet you there in your place of brokenness and honesty. In fact, He is already waiting there for you to come.

Each time you give the Father a chance to be close to you, He wants to draw you to His heart and that is the best place in the whole world to be. More and more of the heartache of your suffering can leave you and the Father can touch you and make you whole in ways that are otherwise impossible.

So often people have tried and tried to get set free and have become disheartened. They have been on a quest to stop their pain, but none of their efforts have worked.

Many of their attempts have taken years and have only ended in futility.

But what I am about to share with you is simple.

It is childlike.

It is the door that you can walk through into freedom.

Yet, I must be honest with you. Not all of this getting set free is fun.

You are actually about to read many challenging truths. Some of them can make a hurting person feel quite uncomfortable because they expose the choices we absolutely must make if we are ever to leave the past behind us and become decisively whole.

But I assure you that as you take to heart the solidly Word-based instructions in "A Trip To Freedom," you will find answers that you have been searching for that will make a phenomenal difference in your life.

If you don't know Jesus Christ of Nazareth or you are not sure that you do, then during one of the moments when you feel deeply moved by what you are reading, all you need to do is ask Jesus to live in your heart and tell Him you want to give your life to Him so that He can be your Savior.

Then as you continue on through this book, you will discover exactly what you need to do in order to live each day as the Father's child.

Now I invite you to travel with me on an amazing journey that took me on a road to freedom that changed my life forever.

Ruth Johnson

Author's Note

In many instances, the use of "he" could be referring to either a man or a woman.

In many cases, the Scriptures have been personalized.

A word of encouragement before you begin this journey...

When I first began my search to become a whole person, God gave me some encouraging promises. He is speaking these same powerful words to you, if you are struggling to overcome the pain of your past and you are longing for a new, happy life…

"My child, I am the one who can set you free from the pit you are in. If you will let Me, I will pull you up out of that dark discouraging place and I will give you a whole new life.

In this new life, I will crown you with My loving kindness and My kind compassion.

I will satisfy your years with good things. I will make it up to you for all the things you have missed out on and I will give you back the years that you lost.

I will renew your lost youth like the eagle. You will be able to rise up on wings like an eagle and finally fulfill your destiny that I have so wondrously planned for you.

Trust Me.

Run to Me.

Run to My love for you.

Passionately embrace My Word and be absolutely determined to obey it. And I will do all that I am promising you.

With My never changing love for you, Your Abba Father."

Psalm 103:1-5 NASB
Joel 2:25 NASB

Table of Contents

Chapter 1   I Need Jesus   17

Chapter 2   I Need A Dad   43

Chapter 3   I Need A Mom   91

Chapter 4   I Must Forgive   111

Chapter 5   Normal Is Not Being In Pain   123

Chapter 6   Healthy Relationships Go Both Directions   127

Chapter 7   Control Leads To Abuse   131

Chapter 8   Love Is Not Taking On Someone Else's Pain   137

Chapter 9   Behaviors Tell The Truth   143

Chapter 10 I Can't Change Another Person   145

Chapter 11 I Need To Take Seriously The Red Flags   149

Chapter 12 My Choices vs. Blaming Others   159

Chapter 13 I Can't Make Another Person Happy   165

Chapter 14 How I Know I Have Changed   169

Chapter 15 How I Know I Haven't Changed Enough   171

Chapter 16 I Am Worthy Of Being Loved   175

Chapter 17 I Must Overcome Being Needy   183

Chapter One

I Need Jesus

Every person has a basic need to give and receive love. Yet too often people choose relationships in which this healthy exchange of love isn't possible. If I am one of those people, I might even tell myself...

> "Never again am I going to get involved with someone who is incapable of loving me.
>
> Never again am I going to let someone abuse me."

Then once again I do what I promised myself I would never do. I end up in another destructive relationship.

Until I was forty-five years old, I was entrenched in this habit of repeatedly choosing abusive relationships. But today all that has changed. My life is rich with healthy, rewarding, mutually supportive friendships. The people I am close to are nothing like the ones of the past who inflicted so much pain.

Only God could empower me with the courage to end my attraction to painful relationships and refuse to allow anyone to abuse me ever again. Only He could give me the strength to rise up and honestly confront those that were still abusive. In the chapters that follow I share the insights that equipped me to make these remarkable changes.

The catalyst for every amazing change that I was ever able to make was God's Word...

**The Father sent His Word into my life to heal me
and deliver me from my destruction**

**It was the truth in His Word that the
Father used to set my heart free.**
Psalm 107:20 NASB
Psalm 119:32 NIV

But before any Scripture could have this profound impact on my life, I had to take the first step.

I had to find Jesus.

My journey in search of Him began as a young child.

My Childhood

I was the third of five children in an Irish Catholic family.

When I was a child, my family lived in the poorest section of South Boston across from a soot-blackened factory and an abandoned, rat infested bus barn. Our home was in a cramped tenement with only cold water and no heat. Each day I lived in dread of the frequent encounters with rats and cockroaches that were everywhere.

Our family wasn't close.

We never did things together and although we were all hurting, we didn't talk about our feelings. We all withdrew into our separate worlds. Even during the hard times we remained distant and didn't help each other. I longed to be close to them, but I was always painfully alone.

My first troubling memory occurred the day I began kindergarten.

I was excited about starting school, but I was also uneasy. St. Bridgett's Catholic School was a long way from home and I had never been that far by myself.

"Mama will go with me," I comforted myself as I watched my older brother and sister leave without me. I gulped down breakfast and quickly put on my uniform. Dressed and eager to go, I sat on the edge of the frayed brown couch in the living room and anxiously waited for my mother to appear.

"I'm not going with you," she eventually yelled from her bedroom.

"But Mom," I pleaded with her, as I walked quickly toward her room. "I don't know my way. Please come with me. I'm too scared to go by myself."

"I don't feel good," she responded coldly as she slammed the door. "You'll have to go alone."

None of my desperate pleas could convince my mother to change her mind. Stiffening with fear, I stood nervously outside the closed door and shuddered at the thought of finding the school on my own. But I didn't want to miss out on my first day of kindergarten. So after a long, heartbreaking silence, I forced myself to leave.

I walked briskly down the street. When I could no longer see our house, I ran as fast as I could until it hurt too much to breathe.

"I hope I don't get lost," I kept telling myself in a panic.

Finally I turned a corner and St. Bridgett's was up ahead. I slowed my pace and tried my very best to calm down.

The closer I walked toward the front entrance, the more anxious I became. I hoped to catch a glimpse of my older brother and sister. That would have been so reassuring. But I couldn't see them anywhere.

Tentatively I approached the school office and was relieved when an older nun motioned to me to follow her. Moments later she left me standing at the open door of a crowded classroom. As I looked around at all the new faces, many of the children were crying. They clung to their mothers who hugged them and with so much kindness.

"I wish Mom was here," I said to myself as tears stung my cheeks. "I wish her arms were around me. I'd feel so much better."

I stared forlornly at the other children for what seemed like a very long time. Then a young nun settled us in our seats and all the mothers waved goodbye.

Somehow I survived the first day of kindergarten, but the sadness I felt from that moment never left me. In many ways, being a child ended for me that day because I realized I couldn't trust anyone to help me, ever again. No matter how frightening a thought it was, I knew that I had to make sure that I took care of myself.

There was one bright spot in my childhood. When I was six years old I had an encounter with God that set the course for the rest of my life.

While I was kneeling at the altar of St. Bridgett's Church, God gave me this promise...

"You will do something special
with your life to serve Me."

I never forgot those words. No matter how much I hurt in my family, I comforted myself with the sense of purpose and destiny that they gave to me. I hid this dream in my heart and it gave me strength and hope.

There were many other troubling moments with my mother.

One of the most difficult times was the evening meal. We ate in tense silence while she sat stiffly at the end of the old wooden table and positioned her tightly clenched fists on both sides of her plate.

"Shut up!" she screeched at all of us if we made the slightest noise.

I winced at the sound of her shrill voice and inevitably my stomach ached. Every night I could hardly wait for the meal to end so that I could retreat into the solace of my safe, quiet room.

After dinner my mother usually stayed alone in the kitchen. I often stood at a distance and watched her lean over the sink while she buried her face in her folded arms and moaned with pain. I wanted so much to put my arms around her and tell her I loved her.

One night I tried.

"Mom, are you alright?" I said as I walked uncertainly into the kitchen. "Is there anything I can…?"

"Get out of here!" she screamed at me before I could even finish speaking.

"But Mom," I pleaded.

"Shut up and get out of here!" she yelled as she whirled around and harshly glared at me. "Leave me alone!"

I did leave her alone. But I ached inside because I could never show my mother how much I cared that she was hurting so terribly.

As I grew older, she became increasingly more despondent. Late one afternoon I heard her loud weeping and rushed into the kitchen. She was sprawled on the floor and crying hysterically.

"What's wrong?" I asked with a frightened voice. "Please tell me what's wrong!"

She just shook her head at me as if to say, "Leave me alone," and kept sobbing uncontrollably.

"Please talk to me," I begged her as I put my hand gently on her shoulder. But she couldn't speak.

I ran to a neighbor's house and banged frantically on the front door.

Minutes later I heard the shrill of sirens and an ambulance stopped at our house. Two men ran into the kitchen, strapped my mother to a stretcher as she flailed and screamed. Then they took her away.

No one in our family talked about what happened to Mom that day. This silence made her leaving me all the more distressing. I fell asleep every night wondering if she would ever come back.

Eventually she did come home, but I could tell she was even sadder.

Now she lay in her bed all day long with a cold, wet washcloth covering her eyes. She always hated sunlight, but now she was worse. She insisted that we keep our house completely dark. Every shade was pulled down tight against the windowsills and tattered, heavy drapes were closed to block out any glimmer of light.

At times I longed for someone to hold me and hug me, but there was no affection in our family. Most nights I lay in the dark shadows of my room and cried myself to sleep.

Whenever I saw other little girls having fun with their mothers, I longingly dreamed of the day when my mother and I could be like that.

"Maybe today we can spend some time together," I often said to myself on the way home from school. "Maybe today she will be alright."

But Mom was never alright.

"Leave me alone!" she screamed at me almost every afternoon as soon as I walked into the house.

"Get out of here and leave me alone!" she yelled if I ever tried to say hello to her. "And don't make any noise. I want it quiet."

I could hardly wait for the days when she walked to the grocery store. The second she disappeared around the corner, I pulled up all the shades and opened the windows.

Cheery sunlight flooded our home and I sang the entire time she was gone. But as soon as I heard her walking up the steps of the front porch, I stopped singing, rushed to close the windows and pulled down the shades.

My world went dark again.

My relationship with my father was equally disturbing.

He was a tall man with bright blue eyes that had a lighthearted twinkle. Yet it hurt to love Pop. I never knew when he would disappear or how long he would be away. He constantly lifted up my hopes, only to shatter them with unbearable disappointment.

He also had a stormy relationship with my older sister, Margie, and this troubled me. I tried harder and harder to be good in order to gain Pop's approval, but my older sister didn't care. She was always getting in trouble and by the time she started high school, my parents couldn't control her.

Late one evening I heard her angry screams coming from their bedroom. I jumped up from my chair and ran to their room. Mom was forcing my sister to lay on the bed while Pop beat her all over her body with his thick leather belt.

"Stop! Please stop!" I begged in a loud, distraught voice as I stood in the doorway.

They ignored my pleas and Pop hit my sister over and over while I sobbed. A year later she was taken from our family and placed in an orphanage. Margie never came back to live with us.

Even in the midst of all this unhappiness, I treasured my closeness to God. He was my constant Companion and my only Friend. I talked to Him about everything. I would even sing my own songs to Him. He was the only one who ever made me feel that someone cared about me.

By the time I was in eighth grade, I was painfully aware of the distance between my father and I. In an effort to get closer to him, I decided to start a new bedtime tradition. I would kiss him on the cheek and hug him every night before I went to bed.

Being affectionate with Pop felt awkward.

It was uncomfortable for him as well. He flinched and pulled back from me when I kissed him on the cheek.

But I refused to let his revulsion deter me.

I told myself...

"Even if Pop doesn't return my affection, I will
still give mine to him.

Showing him I love him is better than no one in
the family loving anyone at all."

Even as I made this effort to build a bridge between us, I
harbored a confusing anger toward my father.

Late one evening it exploded into a fit of rage.

"I hate you, Pop!" I screamed as I stood facing him in the
middle of the living room. "I hate you!"

He didn't say a word. He only stared at me with silent agony in
his eyes as if to say, "I deserve to be despised."

When my outburst ended, my father didn't say anything. He
just quietly walked away from me with his shoulders stooped over
like those of a broken, defeated man.

I immediately regretted hurting him. I never wanted to hate my
father. I needed him. I wanted more than anything in the world to
be close to him. But I never could bridge the dark, widening chasm
between us.

My friendship with God continued to be the only part of my
life that gave me any peace. Being with Him was my only refuge.
His closeness was my comfort in an otherwise troubled childhood.

When I was fifteen, I knew that God was calling me to dedicate
my life to serving Him. As a young Catholic girl, the only possible
way to fulfill that desire was to become a nun.

So throughout my years in high school, my thoughts and plans
centered on that goal.

My Years as a Catholic Nun

A month after graduation, the keenly anticipated day to leave my family to enter the convent finally arrived.

Pop's health was too weak for him to make the trip with me. I stood in front of him, hugged him goodbye and without him saying a word I slowly walked down the steps.

While the car made its way down the street, I looked back. Pop stood on the same weather-beaten porch where I had spent so many hours alone as a little girl. Tears now blurred my vision as I riveted my eyes on him and waved through the back window. When he disappeared from view, grief engulfed me. I never really knew Pop and now my life with him was forever changed. As we traveled further and further from home, I knew that our time together as father and daughter was over.

I didn't want this loss to spoil my happiness about becoming a nun. So I hurriedly wiped away my tears and turned my focus to what was ahead of me.

"I have a new life to look forward to now," I confidently reminded myself. "Everything's going to be alright."

Two hours later, we drove into the long, graveled driveway of the Dominican Motherhouse. I was in awe of the peaceful beauty of the grounds. The walkways were meticulously landscaped and tall eucalyptus trees towered over them in the late afternoon sky. When the car motor stopped, the only sound I could hear was the chorus of birds in the branches overhead.

"Surely here I will be happy," I told myself as I looked around at my new home.

We walked up a long flight of freshly painted steps and knocked on a huge wooden door.

An older nun slowly opened it and motioned to my family to wait for me in an austerely furnished parlor. Then she briskly ushered me into another room and pointed to my new clothes.

When I rejoined my family, I was dressed in black and my hair was hidden under the short, black veil of a postulant. I was brimming with excitement as I said goodbye to them. Then the heavy door closed behind them and now I was shut away from the rest of the world.

Despite all my youthful anticipation of a new, wonderful life, my happiness faded quickly. By the second week I was already deeply affected by being cut off from my family. No matter how miserable life had been at home, they were my roots. They were all I had. I cried every time I thought about them.

This was a semi-cloistered convent so I was forbidden to speak except for a few moments each evening. As I lived each day isolated from the other nuns by this strict rule of silence, a troubling loneliness once again tormented me. Late into the night I paced the long, dark halls by myself until I was weary enough to sleep.

Unquestioning obedience was required of me in every detail of my life and I found this strict submission very unsettling. Yet I complied because this was a part of my daily life as a nun.

Although I was no longer glad to be there, I decided to stay because now I was taught a new understanding of God. He was no longer someone who could be my dearest, closest Friend. Now He only wanted me to do His will and the more I suffered to obey whatever He asked of me, the more I now demonstrated my dedication to Him.

I tried to do everything that God expected of me, but more and more I felt like I could never do enough to please Him.

After six months I became a novice.

My name was changed to Sister Naomi and my hair was cropped short and hidden under a long, white veil. I gave myself wholeheartedly to living the life of a nun. But the ache in my heart grew more confusing.

Yet in the midst of all this turmoil, there were parts of the convent life that I dearly loved. I was allowed to go on long walks by myself in the hills that were a short distance from the Novitiate. I thoroughly enjoyed my favorite haven on a peaceful bluff overlooking the Motherhouse. There I sat for hours at a time reading my Bible and hungrily drinking in the consoling peace that I discovered in that beautiful place.

I had excelled in studying Latin during high school so I loved singing the Gregorian Chants because they were the Psalms of David in Latin. The reverence and beauty of this music lifted my spirit and comforted my soul. Soon I was the one who led the other nuns in the singing of the Psalms.

When I wasn't taking my favorite walks or singing in the chapel, I spent the remaining hours doing the work assigned to me and faithfully saying all the required prayers. But no matter how hard I tried to do everything I was told to do, I was still terribly unhappy.

"God, please help me," I prayed as I wearily knelt alone in the dark shadows of the chapel each night.

"I'm confused. I feel so alone. You seem farther and farther away from me. All I've ever wanted was to serve You. I want more than anything in the world to do Your will. I'll do whatever You want me to do, but what are You asking of me?"

I listened intently, night after night, and quietly watched the votive lights flickering in the dark shadows of the chapel. But there was no answer.

The emptiness in my heart grew more painful. My private agony continued.

All the help I used to receive from talking to God as a child was now gone. I had a difficult time feeling close to someone who wanted me to hurt so much to serve Him.

I longed to find a place where I could be happy, but I was afraid to leave. I was now taught that if I left the convent I would be turning my back on God and I couldn't stand the thought of living with such a terrible guilt.

After a year and a half I made vows of poverty, chastity and obedience and exchanged the white veil of a novice for the black one of a fully vested nun. With a heavy heart, I accepted my extreme unhappiness as the suffering I must endure to dedicate my life to God.

Meanwhile Pop's health deteriorated. He became so severely depressed that he tried to kill himself and he was committed to a state mental hospital. After saying no to all of my previous requests to see my dying father, Mother Superior finally gave me permission to visit him one time.

Pop's eyes flickered with recognition as soon as I walked into his dimly lit room. I stood quietly by his bed as he lapsed in and out of consciousness. His gaunt face was ashen with the pallor of imminent death. Yet despite his weakened condition he was keenly aware that I was with him. He held on tight to my hand and wouldn't let it go.

Tears streamed down my cheeks as the years with my father flashed before me. Ever since I left home, he tried to show me he loved me. He sent me long, encouraging letters and hand painted cards and poems that he wrote about us. In his own way, Pop tried his best to tell me he was sorry for hurting me.

While I stared at him, I reflected on the time I angrily told him I hated him. I still deeply regretted those cruel words.

"Pop, I didn't hate you," I ached to tell him.

"I'm so sorry I said that to you. I love you, Pop. I really do…."

I lingered by his side for several hours and then left without speaking the words I longed to say to him.

He died the next morning and inconsolable grief engulfed me. I buried my face in a pillow and the wail of my loud sobs echoed down the long, dark corridor outside my room.

I wept for the loss of a relationship with my father that now would never be possible. And I couldn't forgive myself for failing to tell him I was sorry for yelling at him and that I really did love him.

After the death of my father, I felt like I was drowning in sadness. There was no place of comfort to run to. God couldn't be that refuge because He was no longer my Friend.

I struggled with an agonizing guilt whenever I considered wanting to leave the convent. Any thought of beginning a new life outside its cloistered walls also paralyzed me with fear. I had no confidence I could make it out there on my own.

But after five years, I finally accepted that I couldn't make the vows of a nun for life. So I left the week before I would be required to make that commitment.

"Soon I'll be back home," I assured myself. "I'll stay with my family so I won't be alone."

Once again I tried to convince myself, "Somehow everything is going to be alright."

The day of my departure finally arrived. I slowly removed the black veil for the last time and carefully placed it on a bed.

"I wonder what the future will hold for me," I asked myself as I stared pensively into the full-length mirror. Gone was the girl of eighteen who was so young, so hopeful, so full of dreams of a happy new life. The woman I now saw reflected in the mirror was a stranger to me.

Uncertainty wrinkled my brow. I had been hidden away from television and newspapers for so many years that I had no understanding of the many ways the world had changed. The strict life of a nun was the only reality I had known since I was eighteen.

I sighed, finished getting dressed and slowly descended the long flight of stairs that led to the front door below. I soon would be free, but I was apprehensive about what life would be like outside the walls of the convent.

Several nuns waited at the bottom of the stairs to say goodbye to me. Each one hugged me warmly and with genuine concern in their eyes.

"Are you absolutely sure, Sister Naomi, that you have to leave us?" my favorite older nun asked as she held me in her arms and cried. "Yes, sister," I assured her. "I must go."

I hurried out the door into the waiting car and I never looked back.

Life After The Convent

"Maybe now that I'm older things will be different at home," I tried to convince myself during the long, silent ride back to where I used to live. "Maybe now we will be close."

But home wasn't different.

My brothers and sisters were even more distant than when we were growing up. They had no room for me in their new lives and my mother didn't want me around. Within days, the same loneliness returned that hurt me all the years I was growing up.

After I lived with Mom for only two weeks, she pressured me to move out. I had no money, no friends, no car, no clothes of my own and no job. Worst of all, I had to face that I had no family and no one who loved me. I desperately needed a supportive place of safety to temporarily stay so that I could re-establish my life. Instead I was forced to accept the harsh reality that I didn't have a home to come back to and once again I belonged to no one.

After many frantic attempts to find work, I found a low paying job that I could get to by bus. With my first paycheck, I secured an inexpensive apartment in a town far from where my family lived. I had no idea that it was located in the heart of the most dangerous neighborhoods in Oakland, California.

Immediately my life spun out of control.

I had given to God the best years of my youth, only to have my dream to serve Him crushed by disillusionment. After I had paid such a dear price to love Him, I felt He had betrayed me.

I couldn't talk to God anymore and the song in my heart that I used to love to sing to Him, now died. When that happened, the part of me that made me alive and hopeful died as well.

I forced myself to drink to escape the frightening chaos churning inside of me. I hated the taste of alcohol, but the only way I could block out the pain and escape into sleep was to pass out drunk each night.

I began to invite different men into my apartment to stay the night.

My gnawing emptiness plunged me into a darker and more troubling abyss. All I could think about was wanting someone to love me.

During this tumultuous time, I met George. He was an older man who was charming and attentive. He quickly won my heart because he said the words I always wanted someone to say to me. From the first night we met, we spent every possible moment together.

He drank heavily, but I didn't give this any thought because I also was drinking way too much.

As soon as George moved into my apartment, our relationship changed. His consideration toward me abruptly ended and now he coldly rejected any of my efforts to be close to him.

"I miss the way we used to talk," I said to him early one summer evening as I lay beside him in bed. I hoped he would care that I was hurting.

"Please talk to me," I pleaded.

He rolled over in bed, turned his back to me and ignored me. I was frustrated and confused by his coldness and got out of bed.

"You used to talk to me," I blurted out. Then I became even more agitated as I angrily glared at him lying there, ignoring me in an icy silence.

"I don't understand what's happening between us...."

With no warning, George leaped angrily out of bed and pinned me against the wall. I was stunned as his large hand came at me. I frantically covered my face and head with my arms as he punched me over and over. My head wrenched from side to side with each forceful blow.

"Stop!" I screamed, hysterically. "Please stop!"

George ignored my frightened pleas. Then just as suddenly as his rage had begun, it ended. I slumped to the floor and my bruised body went limp. I gasped for air as he walked away from me and sullenly went back to bed.

After that night, I couldn't relax whenever I was around him.

Despite such an alarming incident, I still married him.

George kept a loaded gun in a nightstand by our bed and every time I hid it, he found it and put it back in the drawer. One afternoon he aimed that gun at me as he yelled threats at me. That moment was the beginning of a reign of terror. I lived each day wondering when would be the next time he would try to kill me.

I began drinking early in the morning to muster up the strength to face each day.

I added drugs to further block out my pain.

To hide my husband's abuse, I didn't let people get close to me. I was too ashamed to let anyone find out what was really going on in our home. That withdrawal kept me dangerously isolated and I slipped deeper and deeper into a suicidal despair.

Six tortuous years passed.

I hated my husband.

Even more passionately, I hated Mom.

Searing memories of all the ways she had hurt me dominated my thoughts. I constantly relived each painful incident in my mind.

Jesus Comes To Help Me

One bleak afternoon I wearily stared out of the second story window of our shabby, dimly lit apartment. The dark winter sky cast an ominous gray pallor over the deserted street below. I had no hope to look forward to; no joy to anticipate; no dream worth living for. I was only thirty years old, but I wanted to die. Every part of me ached. Feelings of being frighteningly lost and alone consumed me. No amount of alcohol or drugs could silence my desperate, troubled thoughts.

I hadn't talked to God in many years, but I had no one else to turn to.

"God, please help me," I whispered as I buckled over in pain. "I beg You, please help me."

I walked over to the window, pressed my forehead against the cold glass and shivered from the chill.

"I used to be so close to You when I was a little girl," I said hoarsely through my tears. "You were all I had and I don't even know when I lost You. But, God, I need You now. I beg You to be real to me again."

I hid my face in my trembling hands to muffle my sobs, but I couldn't contain the explosive emotions now convulsing on the inside of me.

"If You don't help me," I now cried out in a loud, frantic voice, "I don't want to live any longer. I feel too lost. I'm too scared. Please.... please help me..."

At that moment God's presence filled the room. It was the same comforting presence I knew so well as a child. My sobs subsided and I knelt in hushed awe as I hungrily soaked up His kind presence that surrounded me.

"Ruth, I hear your cries," God told me in my heart. "I'm right here and I'm going to help you. I've wanted to help you all along, but I've been waiting for you to want to be close to Me again."

"Oh God," I prayed aloud as my voice choked with emotion. "It's You. It's really You. It's been such a long, long time since I've felt close to You. I thought I had lost You forever. I've missed You so much."

"I'm going to show you where to find Me," He promised me. "I will take you by the hand and show you the way." Then just as suddenly as He had come, the presence of God left. I lingered there and reflected on His last words to me...

"I will take you by the hand and show you the way."

Hope stirred within me for the first time in such a long, long time and I decided...

"I won't rest until I find God again."

I began to visit different churches of many denominations looking for His presence. Six months went by and my search was disheartening. Finally one Sunday morning I walked into a small church while the pastor was preaching on the story of Naomi and Ruth.

"God loved Ruth," he compassionately explained as I sat down in a wooden pew at the back of the church.

"He wanted to protect Naomi. He wanted to take care of her every need."

Tears instantly streamed down my face.

"Oh God," I prayed. "No one here knows me. This pastor has no idea that my name is Ruth. He doesn't know that my name in the convent was Sister Naomi. Only You know this. You gave him this sermon for me. You care about me that much. You really do!"

The love that God poured out on me flooded my weary soul and I couldn't hear anything else that was said. At the end of the service, the pastor asked if anyone wanted to be saved. I went quickly to the front of the church. As I wept at the altar, I surrendered my life to Jesus.

"I open myself up to You completely," I told the Lord as I knelt there. "I give everything I am to You and I want all You have for me."

I stayed there for a long time while a healing peace flooded my soul. For perhaps the first time in my life, I felt myself relax.

When I left the church that day, the terrible loneliness that had preyed on my mind since I was a little girl was finally gone. The presence of God that I had searched for was now with me all of the time and Jesus was in my heart to stay.

All I had ever wanted was to have someone love me. Now I was restored to the only person who had ever given me that love. I would never walk away from Him again.

"Now I understand what was missing all these years," I quietly reflected as I drove home.

"I loved You growing up, Lord. I wanted to serve You with all my heart in the convent, but I didn't know Jesus. I could talk to You, but You couldn't be close to me the way You really wanted to be. You couldn't because You didn't live on the inside of me. So I was terribly lost."

I drank in the amazing significance of this revelation. As I did, I was radically changed. All use of drugs ended that day. I always hated the heavy drinking so I gladly stopped. I didn't need it anymore to numb my pain.

The dream that God birthed in my heart at the age of six immediately came back to life. I experienced a renewed passion to serve the same God I had dedicated my life to since I was a young child.

Once again I began to sing to the Lord. New, spontaneous songs of love and gratitude bubbled up out of my spirit and washed over my soul like refreshing springs of water.

"Lord," I prayed through many tears. "I never want this song in my heart to die again. No matter what, I never want to stop talking to You. I never again want to push You away. I need You too desperately. Oh God, I do!"

The Reign of Terror Ends

I had high hopes that getting saved would begin the healing process in my marriage. Instead, George despised my new love for Jesus. His cruelty escalated. I became increasingly more frightened by his violent outbursts of anger.

One Saturday morning toward the end of my first year as a Christian, our two young children sat at the kitchen table in tense silence and listened to us argue.

Without any warning, he lunged at me. He furiously wrapped his hands around my neck and dragged me across the kitchen floor.

"I'm going to kill you!" he screamed as he brutally squeezed my neck tighter and tighter.

My arms thrashed uncontrollably. I panicked and gasped for air. In a futile effort to wrench free from his grip, I grabbed at his hands. Then suddenly I went limp in his hands. I was too petrified to fight back. I could only beg him to stop with my terrified eyes.

Seconds later George threw me to the floor. Then with his hands clenched in tight fists at his side, he stormed out of the room.

The children crept quietly away from the kitchen table and took refuge in their rooms. They were too scared to speak or even look at me.

For the remainder of that weekend I lived every second with a paralyzing fear.

"What if he turns on me again?" I kept saying to myself. "What if I say the wrong thing and he tries to strangle me again? The next time he might kill me!"

I tensely waited for the first opportunity to escape with my children. Monday morning he left for work and as soon as his car disappeared from view, I left him.

It took many years of physical therapy and persistent prayer before I was free of severe, chronic pain caused by the injury to my neck. My emotional scars took even longer to heal.

Finding Jesus was my first step toward that healing, but there was much that I still had to learn before I was set free from the damage of my past.

I longed to find happiness. I ached to finally experience someone loving me. But I foolishly thought I had ended my problem when George left. I had no idea that the problem was on the inside of me and this error in my thinking set me up for another disastrous failure.

I was so desperate for anyone to care about me that I chose a disheartening detour and rushed into another abusive relationship. I never even saw the glaring indications that Richard would some day mistreat me. My neediness blinded me to every warning sign that I was walking into another terrible mistake.

Six months after I met him at church, we were married. But to my horror, by the end of the first day of our honeymoon I already knew that I had married another abusive man.

Yet God in His mercy honored His Word. He "caused all things to work together for good," (Romans 8:28 NASB), even this failure. It was within the context of this relationship that I finally learned how to become a whole person.

For the next fourteen years, the Father faithfully exposed to me all the layers of distorted, unhealthy thinking that had been ingrained in me since early childhood. Gradually I began to understand.

All I ever wanted was to be happy. But I finally realized that something on the inside of me compelled me to be close to people who only inflicted pain.

I launched into the challenging process of growing and changing. God never gave up on me even though there were times when my choices made it difficult for Him to help me. Each time I blew it, He reached down, picked me up with tender kindness and showed me how to find my way back to the place where He could continue to help me grow.

That was many years ago. Today I celebrate being alive. I cherish what it means to be happy and securely at peace. My endless detours into destructive relationships are over. And through this book, "*A Trip To Freedom*," all the invaluable insights that I learned are now helping others in their quest for wholeness and freedom.

God set me free.

What He has done for me, He longs to do for anyone who cries out to Him for help.

To every person who is still imprisoned in the shackles of emotional pain, but they want to at last experience this same freedom, the Father speaks these words of hope...

"I set the prisoners free and I give them joy (Psalm 68:6 NLT). So cry out to Me and I will hear you. I will answer you and I will set you free (Psalm 118:5 NASB). For I have paid the price to give you this freedom (Isaiah 44:22 NLT).

Even now, I am saying to you, a prisoner of darkness, 'Come out! I'm giving you your freedom' (Isaiah 49:9 NLT). And I, the Sun of Righteousness, will rise with healing in My wings. And you will go free. You will leap with joy like a young calf that has just been let out to pasture (Malachi 4:2 NLT).

So escape like a bird from a hunter's trap. The trap is broken and you are free (Psalm 124:7 NLT).

Only come to Me with all your heart and this freedom is yours because I care so deeply about you.

I am waiting, with arms open wide because I want to help you.

So please come..."

Chapter Two

I Need A Dad

If we didn't have a Dad or Mom who loved us as a child, we are left with a gaping void in our heart. We will never be completely free of the damage from that loss until our need for the love of a father or mother is met.

As an adult we can't look to our earthly parents to provide this need. They may never be able to give us a healthy, supportive love. Therefore our becoming whole can't depend on them changing the way they relate to us. If we mistakenly believe that the only way we can ever heal from the suffering of the past is for this to take place, we will remain stuck in our pain.

We will keep on looking back into our past and hurting.

We will treat others just as abusively as we were treated and hate ourselves for being that way or we will be attracted to people who mistreat us in the same way that we experienced as a child. We will especially recreate with a spouse the destructive behaviors that we were accustomed to experiencing with the parent who mistreated us.

Inevitably we wake up one day with this cruel realization…

> "The person I married is just like my mother or father.
>
> I'm hurting in the same exact way I felt growing up."

This is a terribly sad reality to face because no one wants to end up hurting just like they did as a child.

In my own determined search for freedom, breakthrough occurred when I realized that only God's unfailing love for me could heal the empty places in my soul. Only His tender caring can fill that dark, bottomless pit.

In this chapter and in the following one titled, *I Need A Mom,* I explain how His love transformed me from a seriously disturbed woman to someone who is genuinely happy. The past has no power over me anymore. This is a phenomenal miracle because for the first forty-five years of my life I suffered such violent, relentless abuse from those I trusted to love me.

God mercifully revealed Himself to me as a very real Dad and the mother I never had. As this new, amazing love came into my broken heart, I was different and I have never gone back to the person I was before this healing love set my heart free. I no longer walk around feeling like an emotional orphan. I live each day feeling special and cherished.

This radical change happened as Papa God's own tender, compelling words exposed His true heart to me. Much of what He revealed to me was initially a shock. I had never seen God in such a personal way. Yet I discovered that He actually tells us over and over He yearns to give us the love we missed out on when we were growing up. He longs to fill us with so much of His kindness that we are completely delivered from the pain of our past.

My breakthrough occurred when I let Him have the place in my life where a father or mother's love should have been. Then He could become that loving parent who always wants the very best for me. As all of this sunk in I became less and less willing to accept what others have cruelly told me I am. My new Papa God helped me to see myself as He sees me and through that drastic difference in perspective, I was changed forever.

How He sees me actually became my new reference point for deciding who I really was and for determining what behaviors I would now be willing to accept from other people. This change empowered me to stop choosing destructive relationships. It also had such a profound impact on me that I began to be drawn to personal relationships with healthy people who genuinely loved me.

To help others also enter into this same transformation, I begin by first exploring the insights that I learned about Papa God because each of us needs a Dad.

Papa God wants to be my Dad

If we had an earthly father who was never around when we really needed him, we missed out on him being with us during those special moments that any young child wants to share with his Dad.

I felt that way as a child and that is why I always felt sad whenever I thought about my father. So many times I longed to share my accomplishments with Pop or just a fleeting moment that was important to me.

But it never happened.

I remember working hard on a lead part in a school play and dreaming about him coming to see me perform. I wanted to know that he was watching me and sharing my world with me. I wanted him to be proud of me. But whenever I looked out at the faces of all the other parents, Pop was never there.

My hopes to share my life with him always ended in disappointment.

Then a miracle happened.

I discovered that God is a kind, caring Dad. I found a healing embrace in His love. I began to experience a Father's involvement in my life that I had always longed for. That revelation began when I found out that Papa God assures us in His own words that He truly wants to be our Father...

"You have not received a spirit of slavery leading to fear again, but you have received a spirit of adoption, by which you may cry out to Me, 'Abba Father.'"
Romans 8:15 NASB

In the Greek, Abba Father is as personal and intimate a name for God as if we were saying to Him, "Papa God" or "Dear Daddy."

"See how very much I love you as a father. I allow you to be called My child, and you really are."
1 John 3:1 NLT

"You are My very own child, adopted into My family, calling Me 'Father, dear Father.'"
Romans 8:15 NLT

"Because you have become My child, I sent the Spirit of My Son into your heart, and now you can call Me, 'my dear Father.'"
Galatians 4:6 NLT

"You shall call Me, 'My Father.'"
Jeremiah 3:19 NASB

*"My unchanging plan has always been to adopt you into My own family
by bringing you to Myself through My Son, Jesus."*
Ephesians 1:5 NLT

*"If your father has abandoned you, I, the Lord, want to adopt you.
I want to take care of you and hold you close."*
Psalms 27:10 NASB/MOFFATT

*"I sent My Son to buy your freedom
so that I could adopt you as My very own child."*
Galatians 4:5 NLT

*"I want to be a father to you, if you've never had a father,
because I am a father to the fatherless."*
Psalm 68:5-6 NASB

*"I would love to treat you as My own child.
I look forward to you calling Me 'Father.'"*
Jeremiah 3:19 NLT

"I will never fail you."
Hebrews 13:5 NLT

*"Look behind you and I am there.
Then look up ahead and I am there, too.
My reassuring presence as Your Father is with you, coming and going."*
Psalm 139 MESSAGE

"Be assured. I am always with you as that Dad you never had."
Psalm 16:8 NLT

Besides always feeling a deep sense of loss because my father was never there for me, I grew up feeling like a mistake. Always from a distance I watched other children laugh and talk and have fun, but I never felt a part of what they were doing. I didn't seem to fit in anywhere. I didn't belong to anyone. Because I was not good enough to be acceptable to Pop, I was not comfortable anywhere I went.

A terrible emptiness from living on the outside looking in followed me everywhere.

Then one day I realized I was no longer an outsider as I went through life. I no longer looked at myself as a misfit or somehow unacceptable.

Instead I finally belonged to someone who made me feel wanted and special. That someone was my new Father who genuinely loved me just the way I was.

This was a phenomenally healing realization for me. It helped me to relax inside and enjoy being me. It had an impact on the kinds of people I wanted to be close to. I was so much healthier now that I was finally drawn to healthy people. And I no longer had to search for someone who could make me feel good about myself. My new Dad gave me this priceless gift and a new life began for me.

Papa God is the one who revealed this profoundly life-changing acceptance to me in His own unforgettable words…

"I have made you accepted in Me, the Beloved."
Ephesians 1:6 KJV

"You now have the free gift of being accepted by Me."
Romans 5:16 NLT

"I call nobodies and make them some bodies.
I call the unloved and make them beloved.
In the place where they yelled out, 'You're nobody.'
They're calling you 'My living child.'"
Romans 9 MESSAGE

"I will validate your life in the clear light of day.
I stamp you with approval at high noon."
Psalm 37 MESSAGE

Papa God will never change how He feels about me

The comforting love from Papa God that transforms a troubled soul isn't here one day and unavailable the next time we need it. It is ours forever and it never changes.

We can depend on this love every moment of every day for our entire life. Contrary to what I had experienced growing up, there is no disappointment in this love from Papa God. He never builds up my hopes, only to let me down.

Once again the Father reveals that this is indeed His heart toward us…

"Place your trust in Me as your Papa God,
and you will not be disappointed."
1 Peter 2:6 NIV/NASB

"With unfailing love I am drawing you to Myself."
Jeremiah 31:3 NLT

"Though the mountains be shaken and the hills be removed,
My unfailing love for you will never be shaken.
My promise of peace will never be removed from you,
because I have compassion on you."
Isaiah 54:10 NIV/NASB

"I will never stop loving you. I will not let even one of My promises to
you fail. I will not take back a single word I said."
Psalm 89:33-34 NLT

"I am placing a new foundation stone in your life.
It is a firm and tested and precious cornerstone that is safe for you
to build on and you never have to run away again."
Isaiah 28:16 NLT

"Therefore whenever you run to Me for refuge you can
take new courage because you can hold on to what I
promise you with confidence. And this solid confidence
that you can have in Me as your Father is a strong and
trustworthy anchor for your soul. It leads you through
the very curtain of heaven into My inner sanctuary
where I am. There we can be close, you and I, and you
can always be secure in My Father's love for you."
Hebrews 6:19 NLT

Papa God hurts every time I hurt

Nothing causes a loving father more heartache than to know that his child is hurting.

Papa God always cared about me in this way.

I just didn't know it.

Whenever I was filled with pain as a little girl, He saw what was happening to me and He grieved terribly every time I hurt. He wept over my suffering just as Jesus cried over the people in Jerusalem. He saw their need for Him, but He was not able to help them because they would not receive Him.

Every time I was abused and rejected, Papa God longed to reach down and help me. He ached to scoop me up into His arms to shelter me. But He couldn't.

He had to wait until I was willing to give Him a chance to be my Dad. Only then could He pour his healing love into my broken heart. These compelling words capture the Father's anguish every time each of us hurt...

"As a parent feels for his child, I feel for you."
Psalm 103 MESSAGE

"I have seen your troubles,
and I care about the anguish of your soul."
Psalm 31:7 NLT

"My child, My child, how often I wanted to gather you
to Me the way a hen gathers her chicks under
her wings, but you were unwilling."
Matthew 23:37 NASB

"I've never let you down.
I've never looked the other way when you were being kicked around.
I've never wandered off to do My own thing.
I have been right there, listening."
Psalm 22 MESSAGE.

"In all your suffering, I suffered."
Isaiah 63:9 NLT

Papa God cares deeply about me

Papa God is not a remote parent who lives somewhere in a distant heaven. He's not a Father who is oblivious to what we are going through.

He is the Creator of all, but He is also our very own Dad. He has the same concern for our welfare that any loving father has toward his child.

He cares about us just as profoundly as the father in the following true story...

A catastrophic earthquake hit a small town in Russia and the shattered walls of a grammar school collapsed. A young boy and all his classmates were buried under a mountain of splintered wood and glass. The people in the town scrambled to reach the children, including the father of one of the young boys.

After fourteen hours, the men with the heavy equipment gave up and left the site of the demolished school. The father kept digging. He was determined to find his son alive. As the hours passed, one by one the people abandoned their rescue efforts and walked away. The father never gave up. Although all others had long gone, he kept searching for his son. During all this time, the boy confidently reassured the other frightened children, "Don't worry. I know my Dad. He won't give up until he finds me. You will all be safe. You'll see."

Thirty-three hours after the violent earthquake shook this small Russian town that father was still digging and searching. In the thirty-fifth hour he found his son and brought him to safety, along with all the children who were with him.

"See, I told you", the young boy said to his classmates as they climbed out of the rubble that was once their schoolhouse. "I told you my Dad would come. I told you he wouldn't give up until he found me."

Papa God wants us to have the same unwavering confidence in His love for us that this young Russian boy had in his father. He wants us to be able to say with absolute certainty…

"My Papa God cares about me just like a real Dad.

He will find a way to help me, no matter what.

He will never abandon His efforts to rescue me and help me."

God's Word assures us this is exactly how He feels about us…

"I have cared for you, again and again, in your time of wilderness, just as a father cares for his child."
Deuteronomy 1:31 NLT

"I'll stick by you when you are down."
Psalm 18 MESSAGE

"When you cry out, 'I am slipping.'
My unfailing love will support you."
Psalm 94:18 NLT

"As a parent feels for his child, I feel for you."
Psalm 103 MESSAGE

"You will not be shaken because I am right by your side."
Psalm 16:8 NLT

"If you'll hold on to Me for dear life, I'll get you out of any trouble. I'll give you the best of care, if you'll only get to know and trust Me. Call Me and I'll answer you. I'll be at your side in bad times. I'll rescue you." Psalm 91 MESSAGE

Papa God gives me a sense of destiny and purpose

A father's affirmation births a sense of destiny in the heart of an impressionable child. When we are young, this validation from a dad builds a confidence that we have what it takes to succeed in life. But without this fatherly encouragement and support, we can wander aimlessly through life, robbed of any meaningful direction or goals.

If we were one of those children who didn't have a dad who communicated that he believed in us, Papa God understands that hope dies within us if we don't have a purpose. Therefore as our wonderful Father, He wants to tell us that He believes in all we can ever possibly become, and He will do all that He can to help us. Most astounding of all, He has the power to help us fulfill what our lives are all about because our destiny comes from Him.

These are the revelations that helped me to understand Papa God's heart as our Dad to encourage us in these vitally needed ways…

"Without My vision for your life, you will perish."
Proverbs 29:18 KJV

"I know the plans I have for you,
plans to prosper you and not to harm you,
plans to give you hope and a future."
Jeremiah 29:11 NIV

"Be glad for all I am planning for you."
Romans 12:12 NLT

"I will work out My plans for your life."
Psalm 138:8 NLT

"I will keep on guiding you with My counsel.
I will lead you to a glorious destiny."
Psalm 73:23-24 NLT

Papa God holds me by the hand

There is nothing more comforting to a young child than walking by his father's side with his little hand reassuringly in his father's big, strong hand.

I never experienced this with Pop and I vividly remember the day when I ached to have that kind of dad. Here is that story…

"Would you like to go to the park with me today?" Pop asked my older sister and me early one morning when I was nine years old.

"Sure, Pop," we told him excitedly and with happy anticipation we walked by his side to the bus stop.

Soon we boarded the bus that took us far from our home to a place I had never been. When the ride ended, the door swung open and we stepped down to the curb.

"I have to go somewhere for just a few minutes," Pop told us. "I promise I'll be right back."

I watched heavyhearted as he walked away from us down the street.

"He promised he'd come back soon," I kept telling myself.

I reluctantly sat on the grass that was still wet with the early morning dew and waited for Pop to return while my sister wandered off to play by herself. Several hours went by and I still waited.

Not far from where I was sitting a young girl and her father came into view. She walked by her father's side along a meandering pathway that was shrouded in trees. One of her hands was securely enfolded in her father's big, strong hand. As I watched longingly, the father picked his daughter up and held her close on his shoulder.

"I wish I had a dad like that," I said wistfully to myself. "I wish Pop was here and he would hold me like that so that I could feel safe and not hurt anymore."

After awhile I grew weary of waiting and walked around the park, but I couldn't enjoy being there. I kept hoping that at any moment I would see my father coming toward me.

Night came and I was hungry. I shivered from the cold while my sister sat on the swings at a distance from me.

For a long time I watched a group of children having a birthday party in a large picnic area. As soon as they left, I frantically rummaged through the garbage pail by their table for leftover food and ate whatever I could find.

Much later Pop arrived.

"Sorry I took so long," he mumbled apologetically.

"Where were you, Pop?" I asked him as I tried my very best to hold back my tears. "I waited so long for you."

"I got tied up," was all he replied.

My sister and I sat in silence next to Pop all the way home. Silent tears rolled down my cheeks as I stared out into the darkness of the night. I felt so lost, so alone and so overwhelmingly sad.

The wound from this incident went deep into my soul. It was one of many times when my father let me down. The devastating feelings of rejection from Pop stayed in the troubled recesses of my heart and nothing could silence them. Yet now this terrible loss has no power to poison my soul. It no longer torments my thoughts. It does not disastrously affect my choices about relationships anymore.

All of this astounding change took place when I discovered that I have a Papa God who always holds me by the hand just like the man did for his little girl in the park. When this surprising revelation became a part of me, my longing for the happiness I saw on the face of that little girl was fulfilled. I no longer felt lost and alone. Whenever I reminded myself that my hand is in the hand of my Papa God, I felt secure.

Most comforting of all, my new Father never lets go of my hand, even if I mistakenly let go of His.

And every time I am afraid, all I have to do is cry out...

**"Father! Papa God! I'm scared!
Please take my hand and help me."**

And He does.

Then peace returns to my soul because my Papa God is securely holding me by the hand and assuring me...

"I am here.
So everything is going to be alright."

These are the Scriptures that opened up to me this amazing breakthrough...

"I will hold you by the hand and watch over you."
Isaiah 42:6 NASB

"I am the Lord, your God, who takes hold of your right hand
and says to you, 'Do not be afraid. I will help you.'"
Isaiah 41:13 NASB

"When you fall, you will not be hurled headlong,
for I am the one who is holding you by the hand."
Psalm 37:24 NASB

Papa God picks me up and carries me when life seems too hard for me

When life gets too hard for a young child, he needs to have his earthly father pick him up and carry him.

This caring intervention from a loving father allows a child to relax inside. It gives him the confidence that he can make it.

The problem is that once we grow up, no one can meet this need except Papa God. As an adult, He is the only one who can scoop us up into His arms whenever we need a Dad to hold us and comfort us.

He can do this for us because no matter how old we get, we are still just a child to the Father. Throughout all the days of our lives, He longs to pick us up and hold us close to Him heart when life is too difficult. In these words He expresses that this is His heart...

"I lift you and carry you through all the years."
Isaiah 63:9 NLT

"I carry you the way a father
carries his own son or daughter."
Deuteronomy 1:31 NASB

"Each day I carry you in My arms."
Psalm 68:19 NLT

If you will let Me...
"I will carry you in My arms and hold you close to My heart."
Isaiah 40:11 NLT

Papa God wants me to feel safe

Every child has a serious need to feel that his father is protective of him and cares deeply that he is safe.

My father never treated me this way. An incident that occurred when I was in late grammar school illustrates why I felt this way...

We were among the few white families in a black project. Our apartment had red cement floors that were always damp and cold. My room was actually an old kitchen with a bed in it and the top part of the door into my room from the outside was made of glass. The project was a dangerous place. Crime, violence, screams and screeching sirens were a way of life for me.

Late one night I heard the footsteps of someone running. The steps came closer and closer. A fist smashed the glass panel of my door. It shattered. A man's gloved hand groped through the opening. I watched in horror as his fingers fumbled for the lock. At first I was too frightened to make a sound. I wanted to scream, but the sound wouldn't come out I was so terrified.

"In another moment," I told myself hysterically, "he's going to be in my room."

"Help! Help!" I finally yelled out in a piercing scream.

My family rushed into the room. The man ran away and disappeared into the darkness outside.

"What's going on?" Pop mumbled sleepily from his bed at the other end of the house. They told him what had happened, but he never came to me to make sure I felt safe.

After everyone left, I wondered if that man would come back to hurt me. Long after my family returned to their beds I lay trembling under my blankets. I was too afraid to move.

That was the night when the haunting nightmares began of a man always coming back to kill me.

After that traumatic night, fear consumed me. It controlled my every waking moment and terrorized me during the night.

If we grew up without a father who cared that we felt protected, we can spend the rest of our life looking for someone to give us that sense of security.

We go on this futile quest because we need to feel safe before we have the courage to face life without constant fear.

Driven by this relentless, unmet void, we establish relationships with people who are willing to try to meet this need. But anyone who is unhealthy enough to be this protective can turn what we thought was a good thing it into a sick, stifling control. And abuse is always just a heartbeat away from control.

The healing truth is that Papa God longs to impart to the core of our being that in His love we are protected and safe. And once again, when we are an adult, He is the only one who can give this to us.

Through His Word, my kind and protective Father taught me that He is this kind of Dad.

He helped me to understand that I can run to Him whenever I am afraid and His sheltering presence will calm my worst fears. I learned that His love is bigger and stronger than any anxiety that can attack my mind. No matter how old I get, in His strong, reassuring arms I can always hide whenever I am frightened.

He is such a safe refuge from any evil that comes against me that He even hovers over me as I sleep so that I can relax. In the safety of His loving presence I can close my eyes and peacefully rest.

As a result of these revelations, a stability came into my emotions that had always been impossible.

A peace began to calm my spirit.

I felt such awe that I could actually begin to feel this new way about life…

**I wasn't troubled. I wasn't scared.
I was at peace.**

In the midst of this transformation, the tormenting nightmares stopped. I realized that I was no longer a frightened little girl inside. For the first time I was a secure, sheltered daughter of the most wonderful Father I could ever hope to have. Papa God extends this same fatherly protection to each of His children. It is of the utmost importance to Him that we feel safe. His own words make this powerfully clear…

*"Don't be afraid or discouraged, for I go before you.
I am with you and I will not fail you."
Deuteronomy 31:6 NLT*

*"I am your refuge. My everlasting arms are under you."
Deuteronomy 33:27 NLT*

*"I am your strong fortress. I make your way safe."
2 Samuel 22:33 NLT*

*"I am your hiding place. I protect you from trouble.
I surround you with songs of victory."
Psalm 32:7 NLT*

*"I surround you with a shield of love."
Psalm 5:12 NLT*

*"While I watch over you, I never get tired. I never go to sleep."
Psalm 121:3-4 NLT*

"If you make Me your refuge, if you make Me your shelter,
no evil will conquer you."
Psalm 91:9-10 NLT

"When you lie down, be at peace and sleep.
I will keep you safe."
Psalm 4:8 NLT

"I will keep a protective eye on you so that
you may dwell with Me in safety."
Psalm 101:6 NLT

"You will pass safely through your sea of distress
because I will hold back the waves of the sea."
Zechariah 10:11 NLT

"I, the Lord, am your Keeper and you are My vineyard.
I water you every moment, lest anyone damage you.
I guard you night and day. You can rely on My protection."
Isaiah 27:3,5 NASB

"I alone am your refuge. I am your place of safety."
Psalm 91:2 NLT

Papa God will never abandon me

If our earthly father abandoned us, we don't have a chance to know him at all. This abandonment can be the result of an absent father or it can come from having a dad who was physically present, but distant emotionally. This rejection leaves a scar in a young child that makes it extremely difficult for them to establish healthy relationships as an adult.

They will see rejection when it isn't actually intended. They will invite rejection because they expect it to happen to them.

Papa God's never changing love for us is the only way this terrible devastation can be healed. He is the only one who can restore all that someone has lost by not being wanted by their earthly father.

He alone can give us the gift of freedom from this damage because He is a Father who really means it when He tells us...

"I will never turn My back on you.
I will never walk out of your life."

He is also a profoundly caring Father who keeps these promises...

"Even if your father abandons you, I will hold you close."
Psalm 27:10 NLT

"Do not be afraid or discouraged, for I go before you.
I am with you wherever you go."
Joshua 1:9 NLT

"I have chosen you to be My own special treasure."
Deuteronomy 14:2 NLT

"I will never desert you."
Hebrews 13:5 NASB

"I never abandon anyone who searches for Me."
Psalm 9:10 NLT

"When you go through deep waters and great trouble,
I will be with you. W hen you go through rivers
of difficulty, you will not drown."
Isaiah 43:2 NLT

"You can say to yourself, with confidence
'My Father is my helper. I will not be afraid.'"
Hebrews 13:6 NASB

"Others may hit you when you
are down, but I will stick by you."
Psalm 18 MESSAGE

Papa God can be trusted

If we had an earthly father who didn't keep his word, we eventually learned that we can't trust anyone. To trust meant that we would get our hopes up, only to have them shattered by a crushing disappointment.

It was easier not to trust at all than to keep having our heart devastated by broken promises.

An incident when I was eleven years old is a vivid example of how I learned that I could not trust...

"Do you want to go with me to the movies?" Pop asked my older sister and me on a rainy Saturday afternoon.

"Yes!" we said excitedly.

"Will you stay with us, Pop?" I asked him tentatively because I still remembered the day he broke his promise to me and left me in the park until late at night.

"Yes, we'll have a great time together," he assured me. I smiled happily at the thought of spending time with Pop and trusted him to keep his word to me this time.

Moments later we boarded a bus to take us to the movies.

The ride took much longer than I expected. We traveled to a theatre far from where we lived. I didn't mind being so far from home because my father was with me and that made me feel safe.

When we arrived, we found seats very close to the front. Pop sat down next to me and I smiled contentedly as I snuggled close to him.

The lights went out and the movie, *The House of Wax,* flashed on the screen. Not long after it began, I realized that it was a scary movie. I never watched that type of movie because I was so easily frightened and I already had so many horrifying nightmares.

I pulled away from Pop and stiffened in my seat. I gripped the sides as hard as I could with both of my hands. The dark sounds of the music filled me with dread. I gasped as a man's face cracked into pieces. Underneath was a grotesque corpse.

I screamed and turned to bury my face in Pop's shoulder, but he was gone.

I desperately wanted to run out of the theatre and look for him, but I was too afraid to move. So I covered my eyes with my trembling hands and forced myself to stay in my seat.

"I wonder where Pop went?" I said to myself with such a troubled heart. "He promised he'd stay with me this time. He promised…"

The movie finally ended and I rushed up the aisle to search for my father. But he was nowhere to be found.

My sister and I waited and waited. Once again we were hungry and tired and we wanted to go home. But this was not possible. We were too far away to even know how to get there and we had no money for the bus fare.

I pressed my forehead against the large, cold window inside the theatre entrance and anxiously stared at the cars as they whizzed by outside.

"Where are you, Pop?" I forlornly wondered to myself. "Please come back…"

Hours later he returned.

"By the way," Pop said rather guiltily. "I couldn't stay. I had something I had to go take care of…"

"But you promised," I said with a hurt voice.

He merely motioned for me to be still and follow him as he walked briskly toward the bus stop.

We sat a long time on the bench without saying a word. I wrapped my arms tightly around me in a frantic effort to keep warm. But no matter how hard I tried to help myself, I could not stop shivering in the harsh, cold wind.

Finally a dimly lit bus pulled up in front of us.

I sat by a window next to Pop in strained silence and turned my face away from him. This time I was too hurt to even cry. My already fragile hope that I could believe what my father said to me died within me.

I knew I could never trust my father again.

There were other times when my father didn't keep his word to me and each incident made it more and more difficult for me to believe him. The damage from this wounding disappointment affected all my choices about relationships as I grew older because I ended up choosing to be close to men who were just like my father. I should never have trusted them, but I mistakenly did. Even though they hurt me the same way Pop did, I kept being drawn to men who betrayed my trust.

Only as I began to understand that Papa God is a Father I can depend on did the cruel wounds from Pop finally go away and never come back.

As I let God love me like a Dad, I experienced that He never makes a promise to me and then breaks it. He never builds me up, only to let me down. As all of this became a part of me, I had the courage to begin to trust others who were worthy of being trusted because my new Dad had given me back my hope.

"Hope deferred does make the heart sick, but when dreams come true, there is life and joy" (Proverb 13:12 NLT). Now I had much joy because my dream to have a Father I could trust did come true!

I also was so comforted by the realization that my new Dad "will never snuff out the last ember of my fragile hope. He will never crush me when I am weak. He will never destroy my smallest hope" (Isaiah 42:3 NLT).

As these truths pierced my very soul, my Papa God "transformed my Valley of Trouble into a gateway of Hope" (Hosea 2:15 NLT). He saw my "hopes when I was helpless and He listened to my desperate cries and comforted me" (Psalm 10:17 NLT).

Ever since I let God become my Dad, I have never been the same because I was able to say with absolute confidence...

**"I know my Papa God.
He will never let me down."**

His own words are what birthed this desperately needed healing deep within my soul where all the destructive heartache used to be...

"I am a Father who cannot lie."
Titus 1:2 NLT

"I do not tell you to ask Me for something
that I do not plan to give you."
Isaiah 45:19 NLT

"I love you, dearly.
Just because your father broke his promises to you,
does that mean that I will break My promises to you? Of course not.
Though everyone else in the world is a liar, I will stay true to you."
Romans 1:7, 3:3-4 NLT

"Not one of my words to you will fail."
Joshua 23:14 NASB

"I will not let any of My promises to you fail."
Psalm 89:33 NLT

"I will never lie to you, nor change my mind.
I am not a man, that I would change my mind."
1 Samuel 15:29 NASB

"Without wavering, you can hold on tight to the hope you have in Me,
for I am a Father who can be trusted to keep His promises."
Hebrews 10:23 NLT

"I will not take back a single word I said to you."
Psalm 89:34 NLT

"Take new courage, for you can hold on to
what I promise you with confidence."
Hebrews 6:18 NLT

"If a child asks her father for bread, he does not trick
her with sawdust, does he? If she asks him for fish, he
does not scare her with a live snake, does he? As bad as
you are, you would not do that to your child. So do you
think that I, Your Father, who conceived you in love, will
do that to you?" Matthew 7 MESSAGE

Papa God is kind and never harsh

If we had an earthly father who expected too much of us, we learned to be too hard on ourself. If our Dad was quick to get on our case whenever we made a mistake or whenever we didn't live up to his expectations, we grew up feeling like a failure.

We either decided it isn't worth trying or we went to the other extreme and constantly tried to excel. In that case, we could never completely relax inside due to all the pressure we put on ourself to achieve, to perform and to even try to be perfect. We were driven to do whatever it takes to earn our father's approval.

My adult daughter, Mary, shares a sad example of how it feels to never live up to a father's harsh expectations.

Her story makes the Father's heartache for every child who has ever suffered in this way...

From as early as I can remember, I felt defeated by my dad expecting too much from me. When I couldn't measure up to what he wanted, I felt so crushed by his disapproval.

I remember when I was nine years old. I clutched my report card proudly in my hand all the way home from the last day of school. As our house came into view at the end of the street, I told myself, "I can hardly wait to show Dad my grades. I know he'll be so proud of me for getting all A's and just one B."

The B was in math. I hated math, but I had worked my very best all year long to earn a good grade in it. I was especially proud of that B because I worked so hard to get it.

"Look, Dad," I told him with a beaming smile as soon as he walked through the front door later that afternoon. "Look at my report card. I did real good. I know you'll be proud of me."

I happily handed it to him, but my smile quickly faded. I anxiously watched as he examined my report card in stony silence and with a serious expression on his face.

"What's this B all about?" he finally blurted out disapprovingly.

"You could have done better than that in math if you had tried harder."

"But I tried so hard in math, Dad. I tried my very best. And the A's. Aren't you happy…?"

I didn't get to finish what I was saying before he interrupted me.

"The B is not good enough," he harshly told me as he continued to completely ignore all of my A's. "I expect an A in math next time."

My Dad acted like I hadn't accomplished anything at all. All he focused on was what he considered a negative. Without another word he handed the report card back to me and walked away.

I stared at him in disbelief as he walked down the narrow stairs and disappeared into the shadows of the garage below. Crushed by his disappointment in me I ran into my room, threw myself on the bed and buried my face in the pillow to muffle my loud sobs.

"I'll just have to try harder," I told myself through a torrent of tears that stung my cheeks. "That's all I can do. Somehow I'll have to try harder."

I was too young to understand that my father's expectations were impossible to live up to. So I blamed myself for never being good enough.

That scenario occurred every time I brought a report card home from school.

By the time I got to junior high, I had given up on school. I just didn't care anymore. I knew that no matter how hard I tried to please my Dad, my very best efforts would never be good enough for him.

"So why bother trying," I eventually concluded.

Mary did give up. Her tragic decision to not try anymore is a sobering example of why the Bible tells fathers…

"Don't provoke your children.
If you do, they will become discouraged and quit trying."
Colossians 3:21 NASB/NLT

Gratefully, Papa God is a very different kind of Dad.

He isn't a stern taskmaster who peers over our shoulder and closely watches us so that He can criticize us the minute we make a mistake. He doesn't demand perfection. He won't crush us with discouraging expectations that we can never live up to.

He is a Dad who knows us inside and out. He sees our every weakness. Yet He affirms us so that we have the confidence to face the difficult challenges of life. He does this because He understands our need to be encouraged so that we can keep on trying.

When we blow it, He extends a father's compassion to us because He knows we need His reassuring love the most when we have failed...

"I made your heart, so I understand everything you do."
Psalm 33:15 NLT

"I understand how weak you are."
Psalm 103:14 NLT

"I know you inside and out."
Psalm 139 MESSAGE

"Others look at your outward appearance,
but I look at your heart."
1 Samuel 16:7 NASB

"I look deep within your mind and heart."
Psalm 7:9 NLT

"I see your heart and I understand."
1 Chronicles 28:9 NLT

"I bend down and listen to you."
Psalm 116:2 NLT

"Just as a father has compassion on his child,
I have compassion on you."
Psalm 103:13 NASB

Papa God only corrects me
because He loves me

If our earthly father abused us when he corrected us, we learned to fear his harsh discipline. We equated being corrected with pain and we dreaded being around our father when we made a mistake.

If this is how we grew up, we never experienced that a caring father corrects his child out of love and never out of anger or with a cruel disregard for his child's feelings.

My daughter's life illustrates the damage that a father's harsh discipline inflicts on a child.

Here is Mary's story…

> I always felt growing up that my father's motivation for disciplining me was to control my opinions and feelings. No matter what I talked to him about, he was always right and I was always wrong.

What I had to say or how I felt was never valid to him. If I didn't immediately agree with him, he grabbed me, hit me or said cruel words to me.

He demanded my respect, but he never treated me with respect and he never tried to understand me.

"You are the child and I am the parent," I remember him telling me whenever I objected to him being mean or degrading toward me.

"God doesn't tell me to respect you, but He commands you to respect me," he always insisted.

By the time I went into junior high, I felt that no one wanted to understand me. I turned my anger toward my father against anyone in authority who came down hard on me.

I rebelled if I ever thought an adult was making a judgment about me without listening to my opinions or feelings. I couldn't handle it at all if someone didn't treat me with respect.

The suffering my daughter experienced is repeated in the life of any child whose father abuses him through harsh discipline.

Papa God is a very different kind of Father. He wants the best for us. That is the only reason He ever corrects us. He doesn't beat us over the head with His Word and His correction doesn't destroy us or frighten us. His presence in our life as a Dad doesn't leave us feeling degraded or abused. He never tries to control us.

Papa God only encourages us to seek Him and be close to Him so that we will be able to make the right choices. He does this so that He can bless our life.

He warns us when we are going in the wrong direction, but only to protect us from doing the things that will end up hurting us. With the true heart of a Father, He only wants to help us have a happy life. For this reason He tells us…

> *"Don't be discouraged when I correct you. I only discipline those I love. I only discipline those who accept Me as their Father. As you endure My discipline, remember that I am treating you as My very own child." Hebrews 12:5-7 NLT*

> *"My child, don't ignore it when I discipline you. Don't be discouraged when I correct you .I only correct those I love, just as a father corrects his child in whom he delights." Proverbs 3:11-12 NLT*

> *"My discipline is always right*
> *and it is always what is good for you."*
> *Hebrews 12:10 NLT*

> *"I discipline you only to help you."*
> *Deuteronomy 8:5 NLT*

Papa God will never hurt me
He is safe for me to love

My daughter shares about being abused by someone she trusted not to hurt her.

When any child experiences the pain she describes, it grieves the heart of our tenderhearted Papa God.

He weeps because He is such a loving Father and it breaks His heart when one of His precious ones suffers such terrible hurts.

This is Mary's sad account of what she experienced...

When I was thirteen years old I was arrested for stealing candy from the convenience store across the street from junior high school. Mom had to pick me up at the police station.

I knew she was upset and I felt bad that I had hurt her, but dad was the one I dreaded seeing. By this time he already had a history of being abusive toward me and I was scared he would beat me up for this incident.

I sat tensely on the living room couch, anxiously waiting for him to come home from work. As soon as I heard his car in the driveway, I panicked.

"Look at what you've done now," he screamed at me as he stormed into the room and stopped angrily in front of me.

He towered over where I sat on the couch and glared at me. His face was contorted with the revulsion he felt toward me.

"I...."

Before I could finish he spit on my face.

Instant rage welled up inside me as I wiped his spit away with my sleeve.

"You have no right to do that to me!" I yelled at him. "You have no right!"

"You're a loser," he screamed back at me. "That's what you are. A loser!"

"And I have every right to treat you any way I want. You got exactly what you deserve. God is just as disgusted with you as I am."

He then quoted Scriptures that proved God supported him treating me that way.

I ran out of the room and into my bedroom as he shouted at me, "You get back here right this minute. I'm not finished with you yet!"

I slammed the door behind me and slumped to the floor by my bed and sobbed. I was relieved that he didn't come after me and force me to go back into the living room.

"I feel like scum under his feet," I told myself as I buried my face in my hands and rocked back and forth, trying unsuccessfully to stop crying. "I'm nothing to my father but a piece of dirt."

At that Moment I wanted to die. I would rather he had taken a knife and killed me than live with how degraded I felt from his spit that I could still feel on my face.

From that day I wanted to hurt my dad as much as he had hurt me. I also tried many times to kill myself. I remember thinking a lot…

"If I have to hurt like this all of the time, what's the point of living?"

Mary had witnessed her father's violence toward me as a young child. When I remarried, the cruelty from her second father now crushed her even more in the tender places of her heart.

Anger and hatred now consumed her.

She turned to drugs to stop her pain.

In her late teens, she lived with different men who used and mistreated her. They always ended up discarding her as if she was a worthless piece of trash. Eventually she lived on the streets of the town where she grew up, troubled, scared and lost.

No matter how much I wished it were possible, I couldn't change the past and erase all her suffering. I couldn't undo the damage. I could only pray that some day God would make it up to her for the years that had been destroyed in her life (Joel 2:25).

When Mary lived on the streets, God often awakened me at night and warned me to pray for her safety. Then days later she inevitably appeared at my doorstep. Underneath the heavy makeup and hardened countenance, I saw a frightened little girl who was desperate to know that she still had family who loved her.

"You were praying for me the other night, Mom," she would say with a haunted look in her eyes.

"I know you were praying for me. It's your prayers that protected me. I would have been killed, Mom, if you hadn't been praying."

Then just as quickly as she had come, she walked away and disappeared down the street. I ached for her, but all I could do was trust God to protect her until she found her way back to Him.

When Mary was twenty-six years old, God answered my prayers.

She became so scared by what was happening in her life that she chose to enter Teen Challenge and return to the Jesus whom she had been running away from since early high school. She was delivered from drugs and the deadly anguish in her soul began to heal.

The days of being consumed by hatred were over. Mary forgave her father and she forgave herself for all her choices that had caused her and the people she loves so much pain.

Then she returned home and began a new life.

Our new friendship helped to heal our regrets for all the years we missed out on as mother and daughter.

Mary found a job, enrolled in college and immediately excelled in both. Layer upon layer God restored to her the self-respect and family relationships that she had lost.

When a child grows up with the kind of abuse Mary experienced, the word father is an ugly word. The very mention of it stirs up the painful thought…

> "If that's what having a father feels like,
> I don't need it!"

If a person is this damaged by their earthly dad, it becomes extremely difficult for him to want to have anything to do with God as his Father. My son John's troubling story further illustrates how a father's abuse can turn a son or daughter away from the Lord…

John was seventeen when one of his best friends was killed in a car accident. Dave was a straight "A" student who was active in the youth group in his church. Even though he was only seventeen, he was a strong Christian and John admired him immensely. Dave was what my son would call "a really good kid."

Many of John's other friends ditched school and partied. Dave was the one who always stayed out of trouble and tried to do the right thing.

Then one day the phone rang. John was shocked by what the voice on the other end of the line was telling him.

"He's dead, John. Dave's dead," his friend told him.

My son hung up the phone and sat down in a chair across from his father. He was shaken and stunned.

"Why Dave, dad?" he said in a loud, hurt voice.

"Why did God let him die? He was such a good person...such a good Christian. Why did God let this happen?"

His father listened in silence.

"If anybody deserved to die, it's me or all my other loser friends who are always pulling stuff," John blurted out.

"I hate God for doing this. I hate Him for letting Dave die."

Without any warning, his father jumped up out of his chair and lunged at John. He was a tall, solidly built man and with all his strength he slugged our son in the face.

"You don't talk about God like that," he told John with livid indignation.

John had been saved since he was a young boy. In his right mind he knew very well it was wrong to talk about God in that way.

But when he poured out his pain to his father, John needed him to understand his overwhelming grief and confusion. At that moment he needed compassion from his dad, not an abusive, self-righteous slug in his face.

John was never the same after that incident. He already had been struggling with how he felt about Christianity because of all the times his father had used the Bible to condemn him. He didn't want anything to do with the God his dad believed in.

I am so thankful that isn't the end of the story for John. He did forgive his father and now he is a wonderful man with a passion for life and a bright future ahead of him. I thank my Papa God for setting my special son free from the past and giving him a new life that is rich with his dreams and his destiny.

To all the sons and daughters who don't want to give God a chance to be their Dad because of hurts they suffered from their earthly father, Papa God longs and even aches for them to know that this is His compassionate heart toward them…

> *"I will not crush you when you are weak.*
> *I will not quench your smallest hope."*
> *Isaiah 42:3 NLT*

> *"I do not enjoy hurting you or causing you sorrow."*
> *Lamentations 3:33 NLT*

> *"I will rescue you and you will no longer be abused and destroyed."*
> *Ezekiel 34:22 NLT*

> *"Never feel like you have to hide your feelings from Me."*
> *Psalm 34 MESSAGE*

> *"I show compassion to you according to the*
> *greatness of my unfailing love for you."*
> *Lamentations 3:32 NLT*

"Open up before Me and keep nothing back.
I'll do whatever needs to be done."
Psalm 37 MESSAGE

"I will never let you down. I'll never look the other way,
when you are being kicked around. I will never wander off and do My
own thing. I'll be right here, listening to you."
Psalm 22 MESSAGE

Papa God wants to heal me

If an earthly father leans on his son or daughter for his emotional or sexual needs, the scars go deep. Troubled, confused feelings come into the heart of that child because the dad he trusted to love him ended up violating him.

My brother is a tragic example of the damage this betrayal inflicts on a child…

> When Joe was born I was nine years old. As soon as he came home from the hospital he was left alone in his crib most of the time. I couldn't stand to see him lying there with no one caring about him. So I tried as hard as I could to give him the love he was missing, but I could never give him enough affection to make up for Mom and Pop's neglect.
>
> As Joe got older, my father developed an unhealthy bond with him.
>
> The more distant Pop's relationship was with Mom, the more he turned to my brother for his need for companionship. Joe was also starved for love, and they grew increasingly more dependent on each other. Each day they spent many hours alone together.

When Joe was in late grammar school, Pop's health deteriorated and he leaned more and more on my brother for his needs. This was a heavy burden for such a young boy. Joe felt so responsible to be there for his father that he rarely went outside to play. He was robbed of many of the experiences a boy his age usually would enjoy because of the unfair burden he felt to take care of Pop.

"Could you stay home with me?" my father asked Joe early one morning just before he walked out the door to go to school. "I don't want to be alone today. I really need you to be with me."

Joe struggled. He was visibly torn. There was a party at school that day and he didn't want to miss out on it, but he also didn't want to let Pop down.

"No," Joe finally said as he hung his head down guiltily. "I really want to go to school. My teacher is doing something special with us today. We're having a party and I want to be there."

With those words, my brother shrugged his shoulders and left.

Pop died a few days after that, and Joe never forgave himself for not staying home with him. From the moment of Pop's death, guilt tormented him.

When Joe started high school, he tried to escape from his unbearable pain by getting into drugs and heavy drinking. He failed all his classes and one day in a fit of rage he attacked Mom. She called the police and they took Joe away.

From that point, my brother deteriorated rapidly. By the time he was eighteen, he was in and out of mental hospitals. Now his violence could only be controlled by potent drugs. He was subjected to numerous shock treatments that permanently stripped him of his original personality.

Slowly I watched the brother I loved become someone I no longer knew. He was alive physically alive, but the real Joe had already died.

"I can't get over that I let Pop down," he explained to me one day when I visited him in a locked hospital ward. "I can't get it out of my mind that I left him when he needed me."

Whenever I was with him, Joe never sat up straight enough to look me in the eye. His head hung low in shame. His shoulders were stooped over under the weight of his overwhelming guilt. I grieved over the tragic direction of his life. But no matter how much I loved my brother, I couldn't help him. His mind was gone and insanity had overtaken him.

He became more and more dangerous to be around and was committed by the courts to spend the rest of his days locked up in high security psychiatric facilities.

Joe never came back to the person he was before Pop died.

If a father violates his son or daughter by using him to meet his sexual or emotional needs, that child may not end up as disturbed as my brother, Joe. Nonetheless, the scars that are inflicted will leave him seriously damaged in vulnerable places in his soul.

No human effort can remove this damage.

The only one who can set a soul free from such horrible pain is our merciful Papa God. He fully understands our shame and guilt. He has a tender compassion for how much we are suffering. He longs to take all the troubled feelings out of us and give us a new heart.

He not only wants to do this. He is the only one who can.

For this reason, Papa God offers His healing love to each of His children who are in desperate need of being set free from the wounds of a father who wanted to be close to them in an unhealthy way. Many have tried so many things to get well, but the Father says…

"Cry out to Me and I will heal you."
Psalm 30:2 NLT

"I will bind up your fractures and heal your bruises."
Isaiah 30:26 NASB

"I will rebuild the ruined places in your life."
Ezekiel 36:36 NASB

"I will restore you to health and heal your wounds."
Jeremiah 30:17 NASB

"I will give you a new heart."
Ezekiel 36:26 NASB

"I will set your heart free."
Psalms 119:32 NIV

"I will put your life back together."
Psalms 18, 19 MESSAGE

"I will make your life complete, if you place all the pieces before Me.
I will give you a fresh start. I will rewrite the text of your life,
when you open the book of your heart to My eyes."
Psalm 18 MESSAGE

"I will pull you up out of the grave and
give you another chance at life."
Psalm 30 MESSAGE

"Only throw open the doors of your heart to Me.
Then you will discover, at that very Moment,
that I have thrown open My door to you. You
will find yourself standing where you always
hoped you might stand, out in the wide-open
spaces of My grace and glory, standing tall and
shouting your praise." Romans 5 MESSAGE

Papa God wants to make it up to me for all the lost years

Our kind and caring Father doesn't want us to spend the rest of our life grieving over what we never had in our relationship with our earthly dad.

He wants to make it up to us for what we missed out on through no fault of our own.

I know this is how the Father feels about us because He tells us so in His own compelling words...

"I will restore your soul."
Psalm 23:3 NASB

"I will make it up to you for the years
the locusts have eaten."
Joel 2:25 NASB

"I will give you back what you lost."
Joel 2:25 NLT

"I will make you even more prosperous
than you were before."
Ezekiel 36:11 NLT

"I will renew your lost youth like the eagle."
Psalm 103:5 NASB

"I will turn into good what the enemy
has meant for evil against you."
Genesis 50:20 NLT

"Comfort, comfort, My child, I say tenderly to you,
Your sad days are gone."
Isaiah 40:1-2 NLT

"I will transform your Valley of Trouble
into a gateway of hope."
Hosea 2:15 NLT

"I will rebuild you.
You will again be happy."
Jeremiah 31:4 NLT

"When you walk through the Valley of Weeping,
it will become a place of refreshing springs
where pools of blessing collect
after the rains."
Psalm 84:6 NLT

"I will open rivers on your bare heights and springs in the midst of your valleys. I will make your wilderness a pool of water and your dry land fountains of water. I will even make a roadway in your wilderness and rivers in your desert.

I will comfort you. I will comfort all your waste places. Your wilderness I will make like Eden. Your desert like My garden. Joy and gladness will be found in you. Thanksgiving and the sound of a melody." Isaiah 41:18, 43:19, 51:3 NASB

The love of my new Father restored me completely. He washed away all of the emotionally crippling pain from my troubled relationship with Pop.

For the first time in my life I had the courage to put my life-long grief about Pop behind me. The tormenting sadness left. The dark cloud of emotionally crippling rejection stopped dominating my thoughts and controlling my life.

With my whole being I thirstily drank in the realization that I was an exceedingly loved child by a very real Dad. At last I knew that I had a Father who was tremendously proud to call me His daughter because He thought I was so special.

I lost so many years going from one destructive relationship after another because I was always searching for someone who would make me feel special.

But none of these efforts ever worked. They always ended in heartbreaking loss and made the pain in my heart hurt even more.

Only when I let God become my very real Dad did this suffering stop.

That is when my life-long pattern of choosing to be close to hurtful, abusive people finally ended as well.

Now it's as if none of that suffering ever happened. All the ways Pop broke my heart don't matter anymore because now I have the most wonderful Dad in the whole world. And He never scares me. He never abandons me. He never takes away my hope. He is so safe for me to love that I can run to Him the minute I am ever afraid.

When I do, He always assures me…

> ***"You can relax inside because everything is going to be alright.***
>
> ***I'm right here.***
>
> ***I'm taking good care of you and I always will."***

Every day of my life I am secure in knowing I have this kind of Dad. In that solid knowing, I have the strength and peace to face life.

Now I rest in the life-changing truth that…

> **Abba Father is my healing.**
>
> **The shelter of His father's love is my strength and my peace.**

Chapter Three

I Need A Mom

I grew up in a home where there were no tender moments of closeness to my mother. I only remember harshness and cold rejection. If God had not become the Comforter to my troubled soul, I wouldn't be a whole person today. The part of me that only a mother can touch would have never been healed.

The Lord sends His Word into our life so that He may "heal us and deliver us from our destructions" (Psalm 107:20 NASB).

This surely has been true for me. Like David, I have passionately felt...

"Lord, Your words have been my only source of hope."
Psalm 119:114 NLT

I feel this way because from the Bible I gleaned the life-changing insight God loves me both as a father and as a mother. When I discovered scriptures that illuminated this truth, and a whole new world opened up to me that I never dreamed was possible for me to experience. A comforting love began to restore the places in my soul that had been ravaged by my mother's rejection.

These truths about the mother love of God are seldom taught. But they were profoundly instrumental in changing my life. For this reason each one is a priceless gift.

Therefore with a grateful heart I have often said to the Father...

**"I rejoice in Your Word
like one who has found a great treasure."**
Psalm 119:162 NLT

If you are hurting because your mother couldn't love you, it is my earnest prayer that the revelations in this chapter will minister to the broken places in your soul.

May each thought help you to receive the same tender love from God that gave me a whole new life.

The Holy Spirit is my Comforter

A mother's primary role is to be a comforter in the life of her child. Yet it is possible for the Holy Spirit to have that same place in our life...

> *"I will ask the Father, and He will give you another Comforter who will never leave you. He is the Holy Spirit. I will not abandon you as orphans. The comforter will come, whom I will send to you from the Father. He will tell you all about Me." John 14:16,18-15:26 AMPLIFIED/NLT*

The Word actually compares the love God has for us to the love of an earthly mother...

**"I will comfort you as a child is
comforted by its mother."**
Isaiah 66:13 NLT

Here are some of the ways that the Holy Spirit can fulfill this need for a mother to love us...

The Holy Spirit has loved me like a mother since I was in my mother's womb

As a child, the cry of my heart was...

"Won't someone please love me?"

But the older I grew, the more painfully aware I became of this crushing realization...

"When I was born, no one wanted me.
Not even my mother."

Because I felt this way all of the time, I was driven to find someone to fulfill my need to be loved. But that hunger couldn't be satisfied in any human relationship.

Nothing anyone did for me could ever change the fact that my mother didn't love me.

Then one day I made this startling discovery...

God wanted me.

He loved me even while I was in my mother's womb.

Before I ever hurt from the abandonment of my earthly mother, He was there.

He cared about me.

I just didn't know it.

These are the words He ministered to my heart to help me understand all of this. They are for every person who has felt that no one wanted them...

"Even when your mother was pregnant with you, I was there watching you, loving you, caring about you. Then I was so excited when you were born that I already had wonderful plans for you.

You are so important to Me that I planned for you to some day be alive long before you were even conceived in your mother's womb. That's how much it meant to me that one day you would be born.

And precious child of Mine, even though your own mother has rejected you, I want you. I always have. You are that special to Me. You are My treasure that I always hold close to My heart."

God convinced me that He loves me in exactly this way through these powerful promises...

"I speak to you deep in your heart
to tell you,' You are My child.'"
Romans 8:16 NLT

"You are precious
when I look at you and I love you."
Isaiah 43:4 NASB

"Even if your own mother abandons you,
I will hold you close."
Psalm 27:10 NLT

"When you were born, no one cared about you. No one
had the slightest interest in you. No one pitied you or
cared for you. On the day you were born, you were left to
die, unwanted. But I came by and saw you there,
helplessly kicking about. As you lay there, I said, 'Live.'
And I helped you to thrive like a plant in the field. You
grew up and became a beautiful jewel." Ezekiel 16:4-7
NLT

"I have cared for you since before you were born.
I have chosen you and I will not reject you.
I'll not throw you away."
Isaiah 46:3, 41:9
NASB/NLT

"I will hold you close to my heart."
Isaiah 40:11 NLT

"I will not reject you.
I will not abandon you, My own special possession."
Psalm 94:14 NLT

"I have chosen you for Myself,
for My own special treasure."
Psalm 135:4 NLT

"Can a mother forget her nursing child?
Can she feel no love for a child she has borne?
But even if that were possible, I would not forget you.
See, I have written your name on My hand."
Isaiah 49:15-16 NLT

"I have been with you from birth.
From your mother's womb I have cared for you."
Psalm 71:6 NLT

"You will be nursed at My breasts, carried in
My arms and treated with love. I will comfort you
there as a child is comforted by its mother."
Isaiah 66:12-13 AMPLIFIED/NLT

"I made all the delicate, inner parts of your body
and knit you together in your mother's womb. I
watched as you were being formed in utter
seclusion, as you were being woven together in the
dark of the womb. I saw you before you were born.
Every day of your life was recorded in My book.
Every moment was laid out before a single day had
passed." Psalm 139:13,15-16 NLT

The Holy Spirit knows me intimately

A loving mother has an intimate relationship with her child.

She is aware of him even when he is at a distance. She understands how her child is feeling, including many of the thoughts he doesn't speak.

God loves us in this same way.

He knows the number of hairs on our head and He understands our every thought and feeling. He is continually aware of where we are. He even knows what we are going to say before we speak…

> *"I pay great attention to you, down to the last detail.*
> *I have even numbered the hairs on your head."*
> *Matthew 10 MESSAGE*

> *"You are an open book to me. Even from a distance, I know what you are thinking. I know when you leave and when you get back. You are never out of My sight. I know everything you are going to say, before you start the first sentence. I know you inside and out." Psalm 139 MESSAGE*

> *"I have examined your heart.*
> *I know everything about you.*
> *I know when you sit down and when you stand up.*
> *I know your every thought when you are far away.*
> *Every moment, I know where you are."*
> *Psalm 139:1-3 NLT*

The Holy Spirit sings over me

When my children were little, I tucked them into bed at night and sang to them until they fell asleep.

One day the Holy Spirit showed me that He also sings over us, just like I did for my children. Through His songs He calms us with His love, just like a mother's song calms her young child...

"I will rejoice over you with great gladness.
I will take great delight in you. With My love,
I will calm all your fears.

I will quiet you with My love.
I will exult over you by singing a happy song.
I will rejoice over you with singing."
Zephaniah 3:17 NLT/KJV

The Holy Spirit responds to my needs with tenderness

When I was a child I often sat alone on our old wooden porch and always a frightening, confusing emptiness gripped me. Loneliness hovered over me like a dark, oppressive shadow. I wrapped my arms around my knees and hugged them tightly to my chest as I thought to myself...

"I wish Mom would come and spend time with me today. Maybe, just this once she will come."

But my hopes were always disappointed.

"I'm too busy," she inevitably yelled at me with a shrill, harsh voice.

Through the years, as I sat on that porch alone, I waited and hoped that she would come, even if it was just for a minute. But she never did. The special times of feeling close to Mom never happened for us and I grew into adulthood with a sadness that would never go away.

Yet that heartache is completely gone.

The overwhelming pain is no longer there.

Now I walk around feeling loved by the most kind and comforting mother that anyone could possibly hope to have. The Holy Spirit is the one who fills my longing for a mother's love and closeness.

This is what I learned that made it possible for this revelation to penetrate into all the recesses of my heart where I used to be so troubled...

God, who loves me with a mother's love, always has time for me.

He is filled with joy whenever I come into His presence to just be with Him.

I never have to beg Him to come and be close to me. He longs to be in my presence too.

When I call out to Him, He never ignores me or pushes me away.

He is quick to listen.

He is quick to draw me close to Him.

The Word graphically captures that this picture of a mother's love is most definitely how God feels about us...

"I care about what happens to you."
1 Peter 5:7 NLT

"I care what happens to you, even more than you do."
Matthew 10 MESSAGE

"I care enough to respond to you
when you seek Me."
Hebrews 11 MESSAGE

"I know the hopes of the helpless.
I will surely listen to your cries and comfort you."
Psalm 10:17 NLT

"I will respond, instantly, to the sound of your cries."
Isaiah 30:19 NLT

"I respond to you as surely as the arrival of dawn
or the coming of rains in early spring."
Hosea 6:3 NLT

"With a love that never ends,
I have compassion on you."
Isaiah 54:8 NLT

"I caress you with My gentle ways."
Psalm 18 MESSAGE

The Holy Spirit wipes away my tears

I cried myself to sleep many a night growing up. They were always private, lonely tears because my mother never hugged me or held me in her arms when I needed the comfort of her love. She never wiped away my tears.

This loss colored every day of my life with a grief that never went away. But now it is finally behind me. I never have to cry alone again.

The Holy Spirit's love is so tender toward me that He even wipes away my tears. Then He saves them because they are precious to Him…

"I will wipe away all your tears."
Isaiah 25:8 NLT

"I keep track of all your sorrows.
I have collected all your tears in My bottle.
I have recorded each one in My book."
Psalm 56:8 NLT.

The Holy Spirit will love me like a mother no matter how old I get

No matter how old we are, we still need to know we have a mother who genuinely cares about us.

If a mother's love has always been missing, the pain of that loss does not dim. It actually hurts more the older we get.

My mother was so determined to push me out of her life that I didn't find out that she was gone until eight years after her death. She forbid my sister to tell me when she died and my sister complied by cutting off all contact with me.

Mom ended her days just as she had lived them, not wanting to know me or even say goodbye to me.

If the Holy Spirit hadn't healed my broken heart, this final, irreversible rejection could have destroyed my mind and poisoned my soul for the rest of my life.

But that didn't happen.

Once again, God mercifully sent His Word into my life to deliver me from this horrendous destruction. He taught me that He fully understands my need to be loved by a mother. He even helped me to understand that I never outgrow this need and that is why the loss of it can haunt us all of our lives.

He also assured me that my face may wrinkle and my hair may turn white with age, but to Him I am never big and grown up. In His eyes, I am still just His child.

I marvel at these words that opened up to me these insights...

"I assure you unless you become as little children,
you will never get into the Kingdom of Heaven. Therefore
anyone who becomes as humble as this little child
is the greatest in the kingdom of heaven."
Matthew 18:3-5 NASB

"Let the children come to me. Don't stop them.
For the Kingdom of Heaven belongs to such as these.
And He put his hands on their heads and blessed them before he left."
Matthew 19:13-15 NASB

*"Listen to Me. You who have been borne by Me from birth
and have been carried from the womb. Even to your old age I shall be
the same and even to your graying years I shall bear you."*
Isaiah 46:3-4 NASB

*"I will gasp and pant like a woman giving birth.
I will lead you down a new path. I will guide you
along an unfamiliar way. I will make the
darkness bright before you and I will smooth out
the road ahead of you. I will do these things and
I will not forsake you." Isaiah 42:14-16 NLT*

The Holy Spirit gives me a place to come back home to

A loving mother can't rest until she knows that her children are doing well. To her dying breath, her overriding desire is that each child find a happy, full life.

Although she feels all of this concern, a mother who has a healthy love for her children won't do for them what they need to do for themselves.

She doesn't encourage a dependency that hinders a son or daughter from making a successful transition into adult independence. But if one of them needs help and it is in her child's best interest for her to provide it, she will sacrifice whatever she must sacrifice in order to be there for them.

At times what an adult needs from his mother is a supportive place to temporarily stay while he re-establishes his life.

At other times of crisis or bruising personal pain, that home is not necessarily a physical one.

It is a place a person can come back to in his heart where he knows, no matter what, his mother loves him. She cares about what happens to him and she wants the best for him. In the consolation of that unchanging certainty, her love becomes a home away from home. It is a comforting, safe haven for his battered soul.

The following story illuminates how all of this was missing in my mother...

Once my father died, life improved dramatically for Mom. Her depression left. She remarried and had a new life with ample finances, a lovely home, new friends and she even took pride in her appearance. Even though life got easier for her, she still had none of the feelings toward her children that are a natural part of being a mother.

The older I grew, the more I was convinced that if I was drowning and she had the only lifeline to throw to me so that I was safe, she wouldn't throw it. She would walk away from me and let me drown.

I never forgot her indifference toward any of my struggles growing up. Consequently after I left home at eighteen I only asked her for help two times.

I turned to my mother for a physical place of refuge when I left the convent, only to have her cruelly push me away. Although I was homeless and struggling to make an overwhelmingly difficult adjustment to life outside the convent, I was not welcome in her home.

She even gave me some pretty clothes to wear and then insisted that I give them back to her.

I was destitute. I desperately needed a mother's support at that critical crossroad in my life. Her cold rejection plunged me into a frightening, turbulent sea of disastrous choices and frantic despair.

Seven years went by and I found myself catapulted into another crossroads in my life.

Once again, Mom could not be that safe place in my heart.

One conversation with her was especially shattering.

I had just ended a violently abusive marriage. In the midst of feeling scared about starting a new life on my own, I was also trying to grapple with the trauma from my husband's recent attempt to kill me.

"Mom, he choked me," I told her on the phone as my voice trembled uncontrollably. "I was so frightened. But I've left him. I finally know that's what I need to do."

She listened in silence to my distress.

I couldn't hide my panic.

"I have no one to turn to," I continued. "I have no friends. I was always so ashamed of the abuse that I didn't let anyone get close to me. I…"

"You'll have to work it out for yourself," she abruptly said before I could finish my sentence. "I can't help you."

After an awkward silence, I ended the conversation. That was the last time that I asked my mother for help.

After that phone call, I failed miserably once again. I had absolutely no one who loved me. Even though I wanted more than anything to finally make the right choices and have a happy life, I foolishly stepped into a second destructive marriage in a desperate effort to feel that finally someone did love me. Only the abuse in this relationship ended up being far more damaging for me and my children.

This was a heartbreaking chapter in my life. Yet today the crippling sense of loss is behind me. The grief from my mother's abandonment no longer controls my life. It no longer influences my choices in relationships. It has no power over me anymore.

Now I live every moment in the sheltering presence of my God.

He is that place of safety that I can run to during the storms of life.

He is that kind and receiving home I can come back to in my heart when life feels too hard.

Whenever I take refuge in that haven, He never pushes me away. I receive a warm welcome and the full, unwavering support of a mother's comfort.

These are the Scriptures that helped me to see that God loves us exactly this way…

"I have been your home forever, long before the mountains
were born, long before I birthed the earth itself."
Psalm 90 MESSAGE

"I am the one who looks after you and cares for you."
Hosea 14:8 NLT

"I will support you."
Isaiah 42:6 NLT

"I will be a sanctuary for you."
Isaiah 8:14 NASB

"Come home to Me, again, for I am merciful."
Jeremiah 3:12 NLT

*"I don't ignore your suffering. I don't turn and
walk away. I listen to your cries for help."*
Psalm 22:24 NLT

*"I'm concerned for you and
I will come to help you."*
Ezekiel 36:9 NLT

"I enjoy helping you."
Psalm 35:27 NLT

*"I will shield you with My wings and
shelter you with My feathers.
If you make your shelter in Me,
no evil will conquer you."*
Psalm 91:4, 9-10 NLT

"I am a shelter for you from the storm and the wind."
Isaiah 32:2 NLT

"I will be a welcoming refuge to you."
Joel 3:16 NLT

*"I am a refuge from the storms of life.
If you are in need and in distress, I am a shelter for
you from the rain. Hide beneath the shadow of
My wings until this violent storm is past."*
Isaiah 25:4 NLT,
Psalm 57:1 NLT

*"Make your home in Me just as I do in you.
Make yourself at home with Me."*
John 15 MESSAGE

"I make a home for you when you are lonely.
I bring you home."
Psalm 68:6 NASB/MOFFATT

"I will bring you home again.
You will return and will have peace and quiet
and nothing will make you afraid."
Jeremiah 46:27 NLT

"I will make a pathway in your wilderness
for you to come home."
Isaiah 43:19 NLT

"Tears of joy will stream down your face and
I will lead you home with great care."
Jeremiah 31:9 NLT

"You will come home and sing songs of joy.
You will be radiant because of the many gifts I will give you.
Your life will be like a watered garden
and all your sorrows will be gone."
Jeremiah 31:12 NLT

The Holy Spirit kept these promises to me.

He restored everything that I lost as a result of Mom's rejection. He gave me back my health, both physically and emotionally. He took my wounded, broken heart and gave me a new one.

He filled my life with so much nurturing and comfort that when I think about my mother, I'm not grieved anymore.

I only feel a deep compassion because by the time I was born her ability to love anyone was already shattered.

Now my need for a mother's love is completely provided for in all the gentle ways the Holy Spirit shows me that He tenderly loves me. This mother love from God set me free.

It's as if all the tragic loss from my mother never occurred. Just like with my father, none of the pain she inflicted even matters anymore.

I am loved.

I am cherished.

I am finally at peace.

I have found a home and a safe refuge in the kind and tender heart of God.

I am free.

Chapter Four

I Must Forgive

No child wants to hate his parents. When we do become so hurt that we end up hating our mother or father, something dies in our soul that we need to be a whole person.

That death remains until we forgive.

If we refuse to forgive, this choice is deadly.

It can cause us physical illness and even thrust us into the alarming shadows of being emotionally disturbed. Worst of all, bitterness creates a barrier between us and the Lord. This is a tremendous mistake because He is the one we need the most if we are ever going to become a happy person and make our peace with the past.

If we persist in our unforgiveness, we give God no choice. He can't be close to us like He longs to be.

He can't send His answers to our prayers.

He can't help us and He's the only one who can.

For this reason He tells us...

"The prayers of a person,
who ignore My Word, are despised."
Proverbs 28:9 NLT

> *"Listen, I'm not too weak to save you, and I'm not becoming deaf. I can hear you when you call. But there is a problem. Your sins have cut you off from Me. Because of your sin, I have turned away from you and I will not listen anymore." Isaiah 59:1-2 NLT*

The Father also warns that bitterness makes it impossible for Him to forgive us when we need forgiveness...

> *"You cannot get forgiveness from Me, without also forgiving others. If you refuse to do your part, you cut yourself off from Me doing My part."*
> *Matthew 6 MESSAGE*

Bitterness is so damaging that it sabotages our worship because God can't receive us into His presence when we have resentment in our heart. Instead He has to send us away from Him and tell us to first take care of the problem we have with someone else and then come back to be close to Him...

> *"If you are standing before the altar in the temple, offering a sacrifice of worship to Me, and suddenly you remember that someone has something against you, leave your sacrifice there beside the altar.*
>
> *Go and be reconciled to that person. Then come and offer your sacrifice to Me." Matthew 5:23-24 NLT*

The Word actually calls a person a liar if he says he loves God and wants to have fellowship with Him, but he refuses to forgive…

> *"You are lying if you say you have fellowship with Me*
> *but you still go on living in spiritual darkness."*
> *1 John 1:6 NLT*

This Scripture captures the deadliness of the spiritual darkness caused by resentment and hatred…

> *"Watch out! See to it that no root of bitterness springs up,*
> *causing trouble and defiling many. For whenever bitterness*
> *springs up, many are corrupted by its poison."*
> *Hebrews 12:15 NLT/NASB*

The word defile has a sobering meaning…

> To contaminate, trample, infect by association with, poison, make unfit for use by the introduction of unwholesome or undesirable elements, to make foul what should have been kept clean and pure and held sacred, to make filthy (*Webster's New Collegiate Dictionary*, p. 294).

If we are so hurt that we feel incapable of taking the first step toward forgiving, there is hope. God promises to give us the strength to make that decision. All we have to do is bare our soul to Him and He will help us…

> *"Cry out to Me for help and I will heal you."*
> *Psalm 30:2 NLT/NASB*

"Cry out to Me for help and I will put you back together.
I will pull you out of the grave and give
you another chance at life."
Psalm 30 MESSAGE

"I will lift the yoke of slavery from your neck
so that you can walk free with your head held high."
Leviticus 26:13 NLT

Forgiving and then making the decision to no longer think about what hurt us is so critical that until we make these choices we won't be free of the past. We can't get on with the rest of our life.

Instead we become mired in perpetually analyzing the reasons why we are still in so much pain. This negative focus can become so addictive that we can get stuck. Then none of our efforts to move on will work because dwelling on past hurts has become a self-defeating lifestyle.

I made this mistake and I deeply regretted it. The price I paid for choosing to hang on to my bitterness shocked me with its severity. I personally had to watch my refusal to forgive contaminate every part of my life. It trampled on those I love, especially my children who had already suffered enough. It infected them by teaching them to hate, including how to hate me. It poisoned their innocent lives.

The following story captures how unforgiveness eventually caused the foundations of my life to unravel.

I had been a Christian for almost two years and I passionately loved the Lord.

I also had received excellent teaching on the destructiveness of unforgiveness, but I still hung on to the hatred that had been a twisted part of my thinking for most of my life.

This disastrous choice catapulted me to the brink of a serious mental collapse. Suddenly my world came crashing down all around me. I heard voices, but no one was actually speaking to me. Late at night I was afraid to walk past the living room. I was sure that a man was lurking in the shadows and he was waiting to attack me. But whenever I rushed to turn on the lights, no one was there.

I often woke up in a cold sweat from terrifying nightmares. In these haunting dreams my ex-husband kept coming back to kill me. During the day a chilling apprehension obsessed me. Every time my children walked outside to play, I shuddered with fear that they would be killed.

After one of these attacks of anxiety, I retreated to my bedroom. As I lay rigidly on my bed, I was convinced that someone was coming stealthily down the hallway toward my room. My heart raced and my body stiffened under the cold sheets. I was too terrified to make a sound. I strained to listen for footsteps, but there was only silence, except for my muffled breathing. I pulled the blanket tight under my chin and stared at the partially opened door.

"He's going to kill me!" I screamed within me as I frantically gripped the blanket. "I know there's someone out there and he's going to kill me."

I couldn't move or barely breathe because I was convinced that an intruder was there. The alarming history of insanity on both sides of my family now raced through my mind.

Then the most frightening thought of all attacked me.

"I'm going crazy," I thought, "just like so many people in my family. I'm going to end up like one of them. I'm losing my mind!"

The evil forces that were trying to destroy me kept battering me with this frightening thought.

I felt like I was suffocating in a dark tunnel where fear was trying to consume me. I tried to stop the downward spiral, but I couldn't push back the darkness that was now overtaking me. My life was spinning out of control and I realized I could easily cross over into a place of such mental confusion that I wouldn't be able to come back to reality.

"Oh God," I cried out. "Help me! Please help me!"

The Father's response was immediate. But it wasn't as comforting as I had expected.

"Ruth," He told me, "you must forgive everyone who has ever hurt you and especially your mother. The hatred toward your mother is the bitter root that is destroying you."

I resisted. Then the Lord pointed out to me…

> *"You have your own sins and failures that you need Me to forgive. And you need Me to completely wash them away as if they never happened. But I can't forgive you if you don't forgive. All your guilt will never go away (Mark 11:25). Your bitterness even makes you as guilty as if you had murdered the ones you are hating (I John 3:15)."*

All of this was deeply disturbing to consider. But it got worse.

He continued to speak this to my heart and quite firmly…

"Because you refuse to let go of your hatred, then I can't help you. You are going to have to forgive before I can let you come close to Me and before I can do anything to help you (Matthew 5:23-24 NLT)."

I was hysterically afraid of what God was showing me. I also knew that I wouldn't make it if He had to send me away from His presence. Yet I still was blinded by my stubborn hatred.

"After all my mother has done to me," I vehemently told the Lord, "I have every right to hate her. I'll forgive everyone else, but I will never forgive my mother! Never!"

Once again God instructed me very soberly…

"If you don't forgive her, your hatred will destroy you and I won't be able to help you."

I jumped up from my bed and stood in the middle of the room. I shook with loud sobs. My mind was already dangerously close to slipping away from me. I couldn't go on living the way I was feeling for another second.

"Oh God," I cried out. "I don't feel any forgiveness toward Mom, but I will do what You are telling me to do. Help me, please, to see her in a different way."

I was determined to hang on to life and my sanity. Like a young, trusting child would reach out to a father, I lifted my arms up to Papa God.

"I forgive her, Father," I said in a strained voice. "In the name of Jesus I forgive her."

At first I said these words completely by faith. I felt nothing at all.

But as I made the decision to speak them over and over, my feelings toward my mother made a surprising change. Suddenly vivid scenes from my childhood flashed through my mind. I recalled her bending over the kitchen sink, moaning in pain; being stiff and white as a corpse on her bed in her darkened room, her countenance clouded with despair; laying collapsed on the kitchen floor, unable to speak; screaming at me, "Shut up! Leave me alone!" every time I tried to talk to her; pushing me away whenever I tried to be close to her.

Then something amazing happened.

My heart began to ache for my mother. Instead of doing what I had always done and just see her as the person who had caused me so much suffering, I was able to see her through the eyes of the Father. Compassion filled my heart for her and Mom's overwhelming hopelessness pierced me to the very core of who I was.

"She knew I was suffering all those years when I was growing up," I finally realized, "but she was in too much pain herself to have anything left to give to anyone. It took all she had to just survive."

I covered my face with trembling hands and wept as a supernatural healing was imparted into the depths of my soul.

"I not only forgive her, Lord," I prayed, "but I love her. For the first time since I was a child I can finally say I love her."

I also faced the wounds from my father but it was much easier to forgive him. Before he died he was sorry for everything that he had ever done to hurt me. His doctor later told me, "Your father died of a broken heart." I knew that much of his grief was from his regrets for failures as a father and as a man.

Once I forgave everyone, I slept peacefully.

The voices in my head were silenced.

The shadows in my home were just that, harmless shadows.

My precious children could go out to play without me hovering over them with my irrational fears.

The days of being afraid to open the door when someone knocked were over.

The poisonous venom of my hatred was gone and the barrier between God and me was no longer there. In all the troubled caverns of my soul where resentment once reigned, a light now shined.

All of this took care of the past, but then I had to learn how to deal with the same wounds occurring in the present.

Mom never changed the way she treated me. Her rejection actually grew more cruel. I drove five hundred miles to visit her. But after I had been with her only a few minutes she would coldly say, "You can leave now. Goodbye."

Each time her cutting words crushed me and brought back the pain from a lifetime of her pushing me away.

The only way I could deal with these new hurts was to be determined to look at her in this way…

I have done everything I know to do.

I have been totally honest with myself about all of the hurtful things in my past.

I have done what the Word of God tells me to do and I have forgiven everyone I needed to forgive.

I have accepted that I have no control over the people who hurt me and there is absolutely nothing I can do to change them.

No matter how much I want Mom to love me, I can't make that happen. I will only be destroyed if I open the door and allow myself to need her love again.

Therefore, I choose to embrace the kind, healing love of God who faithfully reminds me, "As one whom his mother comforts, so I will comfort you" (Isaiah 66:13 NASB).

And I choose to put all this pain behind me once again and move forward by obeying the Father who told me...

> *"Forget all that. It is nothing compared to what I am going to do. For I have done a new thing in your life. See, it has already started (Isaiah 43:18-19 NLT).*
>
> *But if you are going to hang on to the beautiful, new life I have given you. You must once again forget what lies behind and be absolutely determined to reach forward to what lies ahead of you.*
>
> *That is the only way you can press on toward the goal of the upward call that you have in My Son, Jesus (Philippians 3:12-14 NASB)."*

Many years have passed since I learned to take this crucial step. But my mother never treated me any differently.

Even as she faced her death, she had no room in her heart for me.

But I moved on.

I changed dramatically.

Her rejection lost all its power over my life.

I no longer walked around with a gaping hole in my heart that used to set me up for inevitable failure in relationships.

Now I have a happy, fulfilling life and I am married to a man who treats me with a gentle, kind love every day of our marriage.

Each day I am abundantly grateful that I am finally walking in the wondrous purposes of the Father for my life. I am living my dream that He birthed in my heart as a child of six when He said to me…

*"You will do something special
with your life to serve Me."*

I have the best Dad in the whole world in Papa God and a comforting mother in the refuge of His presence.

God has marvelously done what He said He would do…

**When I was a prisoner of darkness,
He said to me, "Come out. I'm giving you your
freedom." And He set my heart free.**
Isaiah 49:9 NLT

Chapter Five

Normal Is Not Being In Pain

If you have a history of choosing abusive relationships, it is imperative that you remind yourself often…

> **It isn't normal to be in constant emotional pain.**
>
> **It isn't normal to be neglected or mistreated by verbal, physical, spiritual, emotional or sexual cruelty.**

In my family I was conditioned to see these behaviors as the way life is and I didn't know it could be any different. Normal for me meant I would hurt every day in some way.

After growing up with so much unhappiness, when I met my first husband I had no idea what it felt like to be happy. I didn't even know what love looked like. Life in my family had only taught me a warped acceptance of abuse.

I lived with George for a year before I married him. During those months, he hurt me physically, emotionally and verbally. He even degraded me sexually, but I still stayed with him. These critical warning bells never went off inside me…

> Something is really sick and really wrong with this relationship.
>
> I need to end it immediately.

Instead, I accepted this man's indifference to my feelings. I was frightened by his rage, but I didn't consider leaving him. Despite his hurtful behaviors, I married him. In doing so, I moved into familiar territory.

Normal once again meant that every day I was going to hurt.

Even after I became a Christian, it took many years to accurately recognize how unhealthy I was in my high tolerance for emotional pain.

Only as I studied God's Word did I grasp that He didn't want me to accept being abused in a relationship that was supposed to be based on love. I learned that He feels so strong about this that He says this about abusive people...

"The wicked are sewers of abuse."
Proverbs 15 MESSAGE

The Lord even tells us not to spend time with these hurtful people...

"You are not to associate with anyone
who claims to be a Christian, yet is abusive.
Don't even eat with such people."
1 Corinthians 5:11 NLT

The longer I walked hand in hand with my new Father, the more I understood these truths.

This new perspective on people changed my entrenched way of thinking.

Now I decided...

> **My heavenly Father doesn't want me to accept being mistreated in any way.**
>
> **Because I'm so precious to Him, He only wants me to be cherished and loved.**
>
> **Contrary to all the heartbreaking losses I had experienced, His purpose is to give me life in all its fullness (John 10:10 NLT).**
>
> **His desire is to bless and prosper me infinitely more than I would ever dare to ask or hope or dream could be possible (Ephesians 3:20 NLT).**

As these insights illuminated my thinking, I finally grasped that accepting as normal the suffering in an abusive relationship isn't life in all its fullness.

It isn't the fulfillment of infinitely more than we would ever dare to ask of our Abba Father or hope that He would give us.

Chapter Six

Healthy Relationships
Go Both Directions

People are destroyed by a lack of knowledge (Hosea 4:6 NASB). God's provision to protect us from this destruction is the truth in His Word that sets us free (John 8:32 NASB).

This freedom includes helping us understand how to stop choosing to get involved in destructive relationships.

A critical insight that I learned about walking in total freedom from the past was...

> **To establish healthy relationships, we can never forget that a close relationship must go both directions.**

To embrace this extremely important truth, we must make this decision...

> **It is no longer acceptable for me to do all the caring, all the giving and all the helping in a relationship.**

If we do interact in personal relationships in a one-sided way, we become a caregiver or parent to our spouse or friend. When that happens, we take on far too much responsibility for the other person's needs.

As soon as we make that choice, we relinquish a healthy consideration for our own needs. Then we mistakenly accept this as the basis for our close relationships...

> I give.
>
> I bend.
>
> I accommodate your needs and wishes and you do all of the taking.

Unfortunately, as a child that is exactly how I learned to define love.

I couldn't stand to see everyone hurting in my family. So I gave and gave and gave to each of them, but I dared not hope to be loved in return. That expectation was futile, since no one in my family could reciprocate my love.

Therefore I decided as young as late grammar school...

> "It is better for me to show my family I love them, even if no one loves me back. Love going in one direction is better than no one loving anyone at all."

That decision set a pattern for all my future relationships.

Abusive men were instantly drawn to my willingness to give them so much and ask for so little in return for myself.

My thinking radically changed once I understood how unhealthy it was to be willing to give in a close relationship and not expect to be loved and cared about as well.

I finally realized that a healthy person is not comfortable being a taker in a relationship and letting me do most of the giving. Only abusive people, who are consumed by selfishness, want to relate to me in this one-sided way.

The following Scriptures opened up my understanding to the truth that loving, giving, encouraging and caring are to be *"one to another"* and not just us doing all of that for our spouse or close friend…

"Serve one another."
Galatians 5:13 NASB

"Accept one another."
Romans 15:7 NASB

"Encourage each other."
2 Corinthians 13:11 NLT

"Love each other with genuine affection, and
take delight in honoring each other."
Romans 12:10 NLT

"Have the same care for one another."
1 Corinthians 12:25 NASB

Even the Apostle Paul expressed this need for relationships to be mutually supportive…

"I'm eager to encourage you in your faith, but I also
want to be encouraged by yours. In this way, each of us
will be a blessing to the other."
Romans 1:12 NLT

Chapter Seven

Control Leads To Abuse

To avoid abusive relationships or to end abuse in a current relationship, it is essential to understand that a controlling person is always one step away from being abusive. As soon as they can no longer control us, that is when the abuse can begin.

Jesus instructed us…

> *"Don't let anyone call you 'Master'*
> *for there is only one master, the Messiah."*
> *Matthew 23:10 NLT*

The Father also added to that admonition this sobering warning…

> *"You are a slave to whatever controls you."*
> *2 Peter 2:19 NLT*

If we allow someone to be controlling over us, we have become that person's slave and they have become our master. We have relinquished to them tremendous, ungodly power over our life.

Whenever we challenge that control, the abuser will retaliate. We will be blamed for whatever mistreatment occurs because to that person our resistant attitude is responsible for provoking them.

No matter how cruel or degrading they act, in their eyes we will always end up being the problem.

In the light of these destructive relationship dynamics, it is clear why the Word tells us that God is the only one we are to give control over our life.

Whenever we agree to surrender that control to a spouse or a close friend, we throw away the freedom Jesus died to give us.

This choice grieves the Lord because He is the One who said...

"I have paid the price to set you free."
Isaiah 44:22 NLT

Therefore to become a healthy person we must evaluate all the close relationships in our life and identify those that are controlling. Then using wisdom and operating in a spirit of love, we must not allow these people to be controlling over us any longer.

We also need to take very much to heart the Father's instructions...

"Because of the cross of My Son, Jesus, you have been set free from the stifling atmosphere of pleasing others and fitting into the little patterns that they dictate.

Can't you see the central issue in all this?

It is what I, your loving Father, am doing, and I am creating something totally new for you. It is a life of freedom." Galatians 6 MESSAGE

"Don't tolerate people who try to run your life."
Colossians 2 MESSAGE

Some of the behaviors that indicate a person is controlling...

We have to like what that person thinks we should like. We have to do what he thinks we should do. We have to be who he thinks we should be. If we differ with him in any of these areas, his attitude is, "There is something wrong with you."

We have to live up to his expectations or he can't handle it. If we are anything less than what he expects, he is critical and disapproving.

He communicates both verbally and nonverbally that we are a disappointment to him.

If we make a decision he does not agree with, he withdraws his support from us.

He displays anger and even rage if we express an insight or point of view that is different from his.

When we ask him for input or suggestions, he is upset if we don't abide by what he suggested. His input carries the weight of a command.

He has to be right in any disagreement, even if it is blatantly obvious that he is wrong, because to be wrong means that he is losing some of his control. Therefore, being right is the most important thing to him. This overriding need to always be right causes him to be rigid, stubborn and set in his ways. These traits make healthy communication and conflict solving impossible.

He is verbally abusive. When his words are cruel and they provoke a response out of us, this puts him in control of our emotions.

He demands that we treat him with respect, but he does not give us that same respect to us. The only opinions he values are his own. The only way of doing things that he genuinely respects is his way of doing them. Consequently, he has no respect for what we think or how we feel unless we are in full agreement with him.

He degrades us in front of our children or other people and feels fully justified in doing so.

He uses the Bible to validate his demanding, selfish, rude, unkind, judgmental, dominating behaviors.

He is self-righteous about his Christianity and critical of our relationship with the Lord.

His interpretation of the Bible is right and he dismisses our interpretation as not worthy of his consideration.

He puts a heavy emphasis on the verses in the Bible that support his position of power and control over us.

Money is power. Absolute control of the money gives this person tremendous power over us. Therefore he uses money to control us. He withholds money from us to retaliate when we don't do what he wants. He uses the possibility of giving us money to get what he wants out of us.

He insists that it is none of our business how money is being spent. He holds a tight rein on all spending. He does not include us in the decisions about how money is spent.

He tries to control what we do with our time. He tries to control who our friends are and attempts to alienate us from the people he does not want us to be close to.

He can't be happy for us if we are enjoying a hobby or experiencing a success that does not involve him. He feels that he is losing part of his control over us. Consequently, he tries to sabotage our hobbies and activities that we enjoy or our areas of success that don't involve him.

His world evolves around his needs and his feelings. If something affects his needs or feelings, he is sensitive to it. But what affects us or what we need do not compel him in any way. Taking good care of his own needs is his highest priority because to be abusive is to be intrinsically selfish. Consequently he focuses almost exclusively on what matters the most to him.

Chapter Eight

Love Is Not Taking On Someone Else's Pain As My Own

We all have days when we need the emotional support of the other person in a close relationship and they will also have days when they need our emotional support. This is a healthy exchange of love.

During the hard times, we may involve someone else in our struggles so that they can be supportive or be a welcome sounding board for our thoughts. But to be healthy we must do all of this with the clear understanding that resolving our struggles and our pain is ultimately our own responsibility.

During those difficult times, a healthy person isn't comfortable letting us take responsibility for what he knows he should be doing for himself. He doesn't want us to feel sorry for him or take care of him. He understands that as an adult he should be taking care of himself.

Before I learned the importance of not allowing people to lean on me with an emotional dependency, I became a magnet for anyone who was unwilling to accept personal responsibility for dealing with their own issues. They blamed others for their problems and I foolishly came into agreement with their self-pity. They hurt and I mistakenly felt like somehow I had to do something to relieve their pain.

This pattern of allowing people to lean on me emotionally began when I was a child.

From as early as I can remember, I was praised whenever I helped someone in our family with their problems. The only time I felt valued was when I successfully alleviated their hurts.

Through these experiences I learned to define love as someone needing me to help them.

When I became a Christian, I continued this learned behavior. I thought I was following the Bible's command to love, but after suffering twenty-one years in two brutally devastating marriages I finally understood the error of my thinking. The following insights changed my perspective and opened the door to breakthrough.

The Bible instructs us…

> *"If one member suffers, all the members suffer with it. Therefore care for one another." I Corinthians 12:26 NASB*

This "caring for one another" means we are moved with compassion by the suffering of others and we are practical in our expression of love toward them. We are the embrace of Jesus to our brothers and sisters in the Lord during their times of unbearable pain. We celebrate with others their joys and we "weep with those who weep" (Romans 12:15).

But I Corinthians 12:26 isn't referring to internalizing someone else's pain and making it our own.

The Bible also tells us…

> *"Bear one another's burdens."*
> *Galatians 6:2 NASB*

At first glance this verse appears to be encouraging us to become emotionally involved in another person's struggles.

But Galatians 6:2 is actually saying…

> *"Help another person with their overload*
> *by letting them know you care."*

It is not saying…

> *"Carry someone's overload and get emotionally burdened*
> *down with their problems yourself."*

This second approach has no power to effectively help the other person. It actually can relieve the pressure in someone's life that the Lord wants to use to help them grow.

In that case our well intentioned, but excessive intervention can sabotage the work that the Father is trying to do in their life.

The Word makes it clear where the person who is burdened is supposed to put their emotional overload and it isn't on us...

> *"Humble yourselves, casting all your anxiety*
> *upon Me because I care for you."*
> *1 Peter 5:7 NASB*

> *"Cast your burden upon Me,*
> *and I will sustain you."*
> *Psalm 55:22 NASB*

The Bible gives us these directives because it is "the Lord who lifts the burden of those bent beneath their loads" (Psalm 146:8 NLT).

Therefore, when someone is hurting and we have done all that the Lord wants us to do in extending His love to them, we need to tell our self...

"I can't fix their problem.

The only thing I can do is direct them to the Person who can.

If they don't want to go there, then there is nothing else I can do for them."

I found it extremely eye-opening that three verses after the instruction in Galatians telling us to "bear one another's burdens," the Bible says, "each one shall bear his own load" (Galatians 6:5).

The message of this verse is that each of us is responsible for our own well-being, choices and struggles.

The different versions of Galatians 6:5 make this point even more clear...

"You are each responsible for your own conduct."
Galatians 6:5 NLT

"Each of you must take responsibility for doing the creative best you can with your own life."
Galatians 6:5 MESSAGE

I now adhere to this biblical perspective in my own interactions with people. When I detect that a person wants to lean on me too much, I don't allow it.

I also can watch an adult struggle and not feel it is my responsibility to relieve the pressure they are under or to find some way to fix their problem. I am now convinced that although they are having a hard time, they are not a hurting child who needs my help. They are an adult who needs to work through the problem them self.

After I have communicated my love and support, I am able to step back and let them do exactly that. Then I pray for them. I also offer encouragement and remind them of my genuine supportiveness when the Father prompts me to do so.

I have found that healthy people want to be treated this way.

Yet, people who have no intentions of taking responsibility for their own problems are easily offended by this approach to their struggles.

Abusive people are especially repelled by wise, Word-based boundaries. When we refuse to allow them to manipulate us into feeling responsible for what they should be dealing with themselves, they often attack with cruel, cutting words. From their distorted perspective, our unwillingness to do more to help them is selfish or unkind.

But based on the insights into God's Word, quite the opposite is the truth. Whenever we set healthy, Bible-based boundaries, we are interacting with people in the way the Father wants us to. We are also protecting our self from getting involved with needy people who will devour our energy and time and deplete us emotionally, spiritually and even financially.

Each time we make these healthy choices and we insist on wise boundaries, we grow.

We experience a deeper peace and a more secure joy.

More and more we blossom into the person the Father always wanted us to become.

And we enter into this coming alive to who we really are without being weighted down by the problems of others that are not for us to carry.

This is freedom and...

"Whom the Son sets free
is free indeed!"
John 8:36 NASB

Chapter Nine

Behaviors Tell The Truth

Watching how a person acts is the way we determine the truth about them.

Yet from a young age my relationship with my mother reinforced in me the opposite mindset.

"Ruth, I love you," she insisted on rare occasions. Yet her words never matched her cold, rejecting behaviors.

At my slightest reluctance to believe what she said, she insisted, "You know I do." I then was required to accept that if she said she loved me, she did, no matter how much she mistreated me. As I grew older, I took this conditioning into my relationships with other people.

For example, when both of the abusive men I married told me, "I love you," I accepted what they said as the truth. It never occurred to me to watch their behaviors to verify the validity of their words. Hearing them tell me the right words was enough for me.

I expected and looked for nothing more.

When I became determined to stop my attraction to abusive people, I realized that I could never again accept a person's words as the true picture of who they are. I now had to be very careful to observe what a person was communicating through their behaviors. Then after carefully considering my observations, I could decide if the way they acted lined up with what they were saying to me.

To protect myself from falling back into the old way of thinking that always propelled me toward damaging relationships, I often reminded myself of God's warning...

> *"Violent people deceive their companions,*
> *leading them down a harmful path."*
> *Proverbs 16:29 NLT*

In other words, abusive, controlling, unhealthy people are frequently excellent talkers who are highly skilled in the art of manipulation. However, if we carefully watch their behaviors, we will see that their actions do not match their words.

The Word clearly makes this same point...

> *"Who people are is the main thing, not what they say."*
> *Matthew 7 MESSAGE*

> *"Doing, not hearing (not just words),*
> *is what makes the difference with Me."*
> *Romans 2 MESSAGE*

> *"It's the way you live, not the way you talk, that counts."*
> *James 3 MESSAGE*

> *"Stop just saying you love each other. Really show it by your actions.*
> *It is by your actions that you will know you are living in the truth."*
> *1 John 3:18-19 NLT*

Chapter Ten

I Can't Change Another Person

To stop choosing destructive relationships, we must decide that we will never again look at someone we are thinking about dating or marrying in this unhealthy way...

> "I see his potential as a person.
>
> If I just love him enough or if I do this or that for him, then he will change."

I made this mistake and I profoundly regretted it.

For example...

When I met Richard, I was energized by the potential for growth that I saw in him. His weaknesses and personality flaws made him even more attractive to me.

He was stingy with his money, but I was convinced that I would try so hard to be good to him that he would learn to be generous.

He was excessively nervous and troubled, but I decided I would be so understanding and kind that his nervousness would heal.

His home was filthy and chaotic to an extreme degree, but I convinced myself that Richard just needed a wife to keep a pretty house for him.

He would be so grateful that I made our home lovely that he would treat it different from the way he lived as a bachelor.

I noticed that he was bitter toward women, but I was certain he would never feel that way about me. In the face of all these issues, I just kept telling myself...

> "He's got a lot of rough edges. But if I'm good to him and if I encourage him, he will be able to make the changes he needs to make for us to be happy.
>
> His problem is that no one has ever encouraged him enough to help him develop to his full potential."

This man became my project to love into changing and I was certain that I was going to be the one who succeeded where all others had failed. And he did seem to change a great deal during the months before our wedding day. But those changes all disappeared shortly after our wedding day.

His stinginess immediately became a major way he was obsessively controlling over every minute detail of my use of money.

His nervousness never improved and as time went on it became so pronounced that he had many symptoms of someone who was emotionally disturbed.

He turned areas of our home into the same dirty chaos that he lived in when I first met him.

Most destructive of all, Richard's disdain toward women eventually included me and my daughter.

From this disillusioning experience I learned how unhealthy I was to enter into a relationship with someone I didn't love just the way he was. I also learned that any changes a person makes can disappear very quickly after marrying them. Therefore it is a tremendous mistake to trust that any improvements in someone we are dating will last after we marry them.

People with an abusive personality are especially good at making temporary adjustments in how they act to win someone over to getting involved with them. If this is the case, then after marriage occurs, the mistreatment from this person is inevitable.

For this reason it is wise for single people to remember that the kind of person someone is on the day before they met them, and before there was any opportunity for them to make a good impression, is who they really are.

To balance out this perspective, as people we often grow as we go through life. That growth is the direct result of the grace of God working in our life and bringing about transformations that are amazing

However it is still tremendous wisdom for a single person to guard against thinking...

"If I marry this person, he will change."

We must be "shrewd as a serpent" and understand what a serious risk it is to launch into a relationship with anyone we are viewing in this way...

"I will love this person into the changes he needs to make."

Chapter Eleven

I Need To Take Seriously
The Red Flags

To avoid getting involved in an abusive relationship, we must decide that we will never again want to be involved with someone so desperately that we ignore the warning signs that this person is unhealthy.

When my first marriage ended, I cried out to God to help me make the right decisions about any future relationships. I had already suffered enough from my bad choices and so had my two young children. With everything in me I didn't want to get involved with another man who would inflict more pain on us.

But I still ended up being attracted to another abuser and as a result my children and I suffered for fourteen more terribly damaging, destructive years.

At first I blamed God for letting me down.

"Why didn't you warn me?" I questioned Him. "I don't understand. I trusted You. I prayed. And here I am in another mess."

But God did warn me. He did everything He could to let me know that I was marching into another disastrous mistake, but I didn't want to see His red flags.

The habit of choosing destructive relationships was deeply embedded in how I perceived life and people. I had no idea how warped my judgment was concerning men.

With much regret, I later realized that during the months prior to the wedding I had dismissed as irrelevant every indication that Richard was controlling, stubborn, selfish, stingy and insensitive to my needs.

Whenever I was with him, all of his behaviors told me…

Take care of me.

Feel sorry for me.

I am down a lot. So I need you to make me happy.

He was the classic needy person and I couldn't see it.

From the beginning of our relationship, Richard acted secretive and stingy about money.

He hated women and he especially harbored a deep resentment toward his controlling, dominating mother.

He was selfish and oblivious to my needs or feelings.

He became defensive at the slightest challenge to his thinking or behaviors.

I did not take any of these glaringly negative messages seriously.

I simply glossed over them as if they were insignificant even though at the same time the Father was trying so hard to warn me that I was making another mistake.

You may be saying, and understandably so…

"How can anyone who knows the Lord be this blind?

How could anyone who is praying about a relationship still marry someone who exhibited all of these negative traits before she married him?"

The answer is simple. I wanted a relationship so much that I blocked out all of the Holy Spirit's efforts to get my attention about any problems concerning Richard. Consequently, no matter how much I prayed and asked God to help me, I was blinded by my own neediness and denial.

Some of the behaviors that are red flags in any relationship...

On my part

The relationship is affecting my health.

I feel controlled.

I feel stifled and smothered.

I'm not comfortable introducing this person to my friends.

I feel used, or worse yet, degraded when I'm around him.

I don't feel free to be completely myself when I'm around him.

I don't feel like I can totally relax and let my hair down with him.

I find myself frequently walking on eggshells when I'm around him. I am concerned about how he will react to me.

I protect him from my true feelings. In doing so, I act like he is a child who cannot handle my honest feelings.

I allow him to be dominating over me and tell me what to do. In doing so, I am acting as a child and allowing this person to relate to me as a parent.

I'm becoming so emotionally involved with his problems that I'm feeling burdened by them. I feel a responsibility to help him fix his problems.

I make excuses for his behaviors to other people and to myself.

I find myself becoming more and more isolated from people who are close to me.

On his part

He does not take it to heart when I tell him that his behaviors toward me are hurtful, troubling or unkind.

He is demanding.

He expects me to wait on him.

He bristles if I ask him to help me.

He is stingy. He is extremely private about his money.

He is selfish and self-centered.

He is oblivious to my feelings or needs.

He is dominating.

He is moody.

He exhibits anti-social behavior around other people.

He has sudden mood swings and unpredictable behaviors.

He is easily upset by annoyances that are a part of daily life.

He is emotionally dependent on me. He leans on me for his emotional needs instead of taking responsibility for them himself.

He is often depressed. He frequently expresses a gloomy, negative perspective about life.

He does not like himself. He is insecure in who he is.

His self-confidence is so shaky, my strengths and my successes easily threaten him.

He does most of the talking in our conversations. He does not reciprocate by making it a priority to listen to me.

He is sullen and quiet. He is non-communicative and buries his true feelings deep inside of him.

He has a quick excuse for being rude, unkind or selfish.

He explains away negative behaviors and expects me to accept his rationalizations and excuses.

He dwells on past relationships and past hurts. He has not let go of the hurts of the past. He is bitter. He is a grudge holder.

He is quick to blame others for his past problems and does not take responsibility for them himself.

He is quick to blame me if we have problems. Everything is always somehow my fault.

His response to conflict between us is to be defensive, to verbally attack me, refuse to listen to me, shut down on me emotionally or shut me out.

He makes promises, but he does not keep his word to me.

He says he is a Christian. He talks about Jesus. But there is no fruit in his life. He is not walking his talk.

He feels inadequate a lot of the time. I find myself constantly in the role of reassuring him, encouraging him, pumping up his low self-worth.

He is looking for someone to rescue him from his situation or personal problems.

He is looking for someone to take care of him.

He is critical of me.

He wants to change me.

He puts me down, privately or in front of other people.

He is jealous of my time with other people.

He pressures me to distance myself from my support system, such as friends, co-workers, and family members, especially those who might be warning me that he is abusing me or if getting involved with him is a mistake.

He has to be in control.

He insists on helping me make personal decisions.

He tries to control what I do with my money.

He tries to control whom I spend my time with.

He loses his temper easily. When he does, I feel uneasy.

It has crossed my mind that due to the intensity of his anger, he could be someone whose anger could get out of control. That thought is scary to me.

He breaks, throws or strikes objects, when he gets angry.

He has hit other people in the past and has excuses why they pushed him over the edge.

Although he hasn't physically hit me, he makes verbal threats of violence, such as, "I'll slap you."

He has hit me and is profusely sorry. He promises it will never happen again.

As a couple

Physical pleasure in the relationship is the number one focus. No real friendship is developing.

We have very little in common in our goals or interests. We are mainly opposites in the way we think, which in a marriage will give us an endless amount of issues to argue about.

Once we decide to listen to the Holy Spirit alerting us with His warning signals about a relationship, we need to remember that God cautions us…

"Be shrewd as serpents and innocent as doves."
Matthew 10:16 NASB

This godly shrewdness is the diametric opposite of denial.

Denial blinds us to the way things really are. It is "a refusal to admit the truth" (*Webster's,* p. 300). It causes us to create our own reality that is far removed from the way things really are.

Therefore, to "be shrewd as a serpent" in relationships, we need to face head on any shred of denial that is operating in our thinking.

God wants to help us make this transition out of denial into sound judgment. And as long as we are willing to listen to Him, He is more than able to reveal to us insights about life and people that we are not able to see on our own.

If we ever revert back to our old habit of blocking out objective reality, Papa God is always available to guide us get back to the truth if we face this mistake and cry out to Him for His wisdom.

Each time we open ourselves up to the Father in this honest way, He will give us every discernment we need to see another person for who he really is. He will gladly help us succeed in the changes we are trying to make.

We simply must be willing to listen to Him and never dismiss as unimportant when He gives us a lack of peace.

Then in all situations we must act on what He shows us.

These commitments on our part will allow the Lord to keep on exposing to us the blind spots in our thinking. Then He is able to lead us in the direction of His very best for us.

It is so reassuring that the Father makes the following promises that He will provide us with all this help...

"My revelation is whole and pulls your life together.
My signposts are clear and point out the right road.
My life-maps are right, showing you the way to joy.
My directions are plain."
Psalm 19 MESSAGE

"I correct the misdirected and
send them in the right direction."
Psalm 25 MESSAGE

"Listen for My Voice in everything you do, everywhere
you go. I am the one who will keep you on track."
Proverbs 3 MESSAGE

"Call out to Me and I will answer you.
I will answer you by revealing to you what is hard and
hidden, those things that you do not know."
Jeremiah 33:3 MOFFATT

"I will guide you along the best pathway for your life.
I will advise you and watch over you."
Psalm 32:8 NLT

"You belong to Me.
I am holding your right hand.
I will keep on guiding you with My counsel.
I will lead you to a glorious destiny."
Psalm 73:23-24 NLT

Chapter Twelve

My Choices vs. Blaming Others

Innocent, defenseless children suffer because of the sins against them by their father or mother (Jeremiah 32:18 NLT). Their suffering can be devastating and even tragic. It can damage them for the rest of their lives.

I definitely was one of those children and I spent years searching for answers to resolve my heartache. I longed to live the breakthrough that Paul wrote about when he said he was able to forget the past and embrace his future in Jesus (Philippians 3:13-14 NASB).

No matter how many setbacks I encountered along the way, I sincerely wanted to make this remarkable transition and finally overcome the emotional pain that always defeated me. Despite wanting this so earnestly, I ended up in frustrating ditches. With the best of intentions, I repeatedly chose detours that devoured precious years of my life.

After floundering in an endless maze of confusing dead-ends, I finally understood two simple truths that somehow had always escaped me. Grasping them was a major step toward being set free of my crippling shackles.

The first revelation was…

> **I can't change what happened to me in the past.**

> **I only have the power to choose how I will respond to it in the present.**

That choice is what determines if I am going to daily experience being blessed or bringing upon myself much unhappiness. The Father states this truth very clearly…

"Now listen. Today I am giving you a choice between prosperity and disaster. I set before you life and death, the blessing and the curse. So choose life in order that you may live, you and your descendants." Deuteronomy 30:15,19 NLT/NASB

The second revelation was…

**People can only do to me
what I allow them to do.**

There are traumatic things that happen to adults over which they have no control, such as when a person is raped. These are adult victims who must not feel responsible for what was forced on them.

So when I say that people can only do to us what we allow them to do, I am referring to the fact that as I grew older I blamed my problems on what my mother or father did to me as a child. But the truth was I kept paying a heavy price for what I was allowing others to inflict on me in the present.

For example…

What I suffered in my two abusive marriages would never have occurred if I had not allowed those two men to be cruel to me.

No one made me endure being mistreated by them. It was my own unhealthy decision to accept it.

A major breakthrough occurred in my journey toward wholeness as soon as I stopped blaming people for what they had done to me and I honestly faced this uncomfortable, but life defining truth...

To end the pain from my past, I must be willing to admit that if my life is a mess, it isn't because of someone else.

It is the result of my own wrong choices.

As a result of this significant change in my thinking, I stopped looking at myself as a victim and immediately began to take full responsibility for my own adult decisions. Then I began to make amazing new choices in my personal relationships.

The following are some of the decisions I realized I must make so that a new world of becoming more and more a whole person could open up to me...

I can choose to forgive.

I can stop rehearsing in my mind the hurts of the past.

I can make a dedicated effort to obey God's instruction to fix my thoughts on what is pure, lovely and admirable. I can discipline myself to think about what is a good report and is worthy of praise (Philippians 4:8 NLT).

I can be committed to learn about my authority as a believer and stop letting Satan beat me up with his attacks and his determined, demonic oppression.

I can choose to make it a high priority to get to know God as my real Dad and as my Comforter.

I can diligently study God's Word and hide carefully in my heart everything He says about who I am and who He really is. Then I can consciously decide that my new identity is based completely on who my Abba Father tells me I am and no longer on the voices of the past.

I also realized that to be healthy I had to consider the choices I had the freedom to make that could continue to destroy me...

Those destructive decisions are...

I can neglect times of fellowship and intimacy with God.

I can make it a low priority to study His Word.

I can neglect to exercise my authority as a believer.

I can choose to be isolated from fellowship with God's people.

I can decide to hang on to my bitterness that I am convinced I have every right to feel.

I can continue to define who I am through the words of those who mistreated me.

I can continue with my life-long habit of thinking about every rotten thing that has ever happened to me.

I can continue to dwell on negative thoughts.

I can keep on rehearsing in my mind all the things that people had done to hurt me.

I can keep on spending time thinking about things that scared me.

I can continue to allow people to be abusive, cruel and controlling toward me and then I can keep on blaming them for all the misery in my life.

I finally faced that if these were my decisions, I only prolonged my suffering and I had done it to myself.

When my first abusive marriage ended, I didn't have these insights. I mistakenly told myself...

"I just got rid of my problem. My abusive husband is out of my life. Now I will be happy."

Within a year I remarried.

This marriage proved to be far more damaging than the first one. Even though I convinced myself that I had learned enough to make the right choice about another relationship, I ended up in another abusive marriage. The only difference was that my first husband beat me with his fists. The blows from my second husband were his relentlessly cruel, degrading words toward me and my children.

When this destructive marriage ended fourteen years later, my attitude was radically different. I no longer thought that my problem was this man.

Now I understood that the problem was inside of me and it was rooted in why I chose to marry such an unhealthy person in the first place. So I asked the Lord to answer these critical questions...

"Why have I always been attracted to cruel men?
Why have they always been attracted to me?"

As I cried out to the Father to give me understanding, all that mattered was that I fully grasp how to end my life-long pattern of being drawn to people who were incapable of loving me.

My thoughts were no longer focused on blaming someone else. I no longer saw myself as a victim. Now I was only determined to make sure I understood how I still needed to grow so that my past would never again have the power to dictate my future.

If I had not made this change, I would not have been ready for the happy, rewarding, fulfilling relationship I have with my husband, Barry. When he met me, he was a delightfully healthy person. He wanted to enjoy life and have fun with someone who could share the present with him and walk into a wonderful future with him.

Therefore, on the day we met, if I was still mired in looking back into the hurts of my past, this negative, unhappy focus would have killed our relationship before it even had a chance to begin. Barry may have spent one time with me. But if this is what I was still like, he later told me...

"The last thing in the world I was looking for was someone who still needed to focus on her past.

I would not have been interested in getting to know you if that is the way you were when I met you."

Chapter Thirteen

I Can't Make Another Person Happy

To function in a healthy way in any relationship, we must remind ourself that it is not our responsibility to make another person happy.

A person who is chronically miserable and consistently views life from a negative perspective often has the expectation that somehow it is our responsibility to do something to make them happy. But any efforts we invest to improve their happiness level will have the same impact as if we put water into a bucket with holes in it. As fast as we pour into that person, whatever good they experience from our efforts quickly drains out of them.

Soon they are right back where they started and they expect us to do something about it.

This same principle applies to us. It is not the responsibility of anyone else to make us happy.

Happiness is something that we need to find within our own heart and spirit toward ourself.

This perspective about ourselves comes from letting God get through to us, on a daily basis, how tenderly and deeply He loves us.

It comes from reminding ourself often that no matter what the circumstances are that surround us, this is how the Lord feels about us...

I am precious to Him.

I am special.

I am of such value and worth that Jesus left the Father, came to earth and died an excruciatingly horrible death so that I could know His love and find wholeness and peace in Him.

God tells us that this is exactly how He feels about us...

"You are precious to Me.
You are honored and I love you."
Isaiah 43:4 NLT

"I have chosen you for Myself, for My own
special treasure."
Psalm 135:4 NLT

"You are close to My heart."
Psalm 148:14 NIV

"I declare today that you are My own special treasure."
Deuteronomy 26:18 NLT

If our happiness is based on how people feel about us, our emotions will rise and fall with all the variations in our relationships. But if it is rooted in God's unchanging love for us, our joy weathers the storms of life and we are protected by an amazing peace.

No matter what happens in any of our relationships, with absolute certainty we can always come back to these truths…

I am special to the Lord.

I am totally and absolutely loved by our Papa God.

No matter what I'm a treasure to Him.

For most of my life, it was impossible for me to feel this way about myself or about God.

For example…

When I met my second husband, I was a single mother with the full responsibility of providing for two young children. My first husband had disappeared shortly after the marriage ended and I had no financial support. Having been a stay-at-home mom during the marriage, I had no skills to get a job that would provide me with an adequate income.

I mistakenly wanted my prince charming to come along, rescue me from these pressures and make me happy.

I didn't slow down and let God teach me how to grow as a person so that I could effectively deal with caring for myself and my children.

I never even gave Him a chance to show me how to find happiness through His love for me.

I foolishly thought a relationship was the solution to my problems. Because I wanted a man to come into my life who could make me happy, I rushed into a second marriage.

By the time that relationship ended fourteen years later, I had grown tremendously. I was no longer willing to accept responsibility for making someone else happy and I didn't expect someone else to do that for me.

Now I understood that other people can only enhance the happiness I've already found within myself.

This breakthrough was birthed in my heart when I realized I was so loved by my wonderful, new Father the Lord that I no longer needed to look to someone else for my sense of well-being. It now came from an ever-present awareness of Papa God's tender, protective, caring for me.

All of my life I had lived on an emotional roller coaster whenever I experienced the slightest rejection. But now His constant love for me became the basis for a new emotional stability.

Life can still hurt tremendously at times.

But I have a Dad to help me find my way back to where I am once again at peace.

Before Papa God became my Father, I could never find my way there.

Chapter Fourteen

How I Know I've Changed

There are behaviors and ways of thinking about life and people that become an integral part of our lifestyle when we embrace the practical instructions in God's Word and we receive the very real love of Abba Father into our hearts.

These changes empower us to make healthy relationship choices.

Some of the ways I can tell I've changed enough to make the right choices about relationships...

I like who I am.

I have developed a healthy level of independence.

I have a strong confidence that with God's help I can take care of my own needs. I'm not looking for someone to take care of me.

I don't have to be in a relationship to be happy and to feel like a whole, complete person.

I can thoroughly enjoy the time I spend alone with myself, at least most of the time.

I have developed my own interests and hobbies.

I have non-romantic friends with whom I can have fun.

I have my own dreams and goals and I am taking practical steps toward accomplishing them.

The kind of needy, controlling people who used to be drawn to me are not attracted to me anymore.

I don't feel it is selfish for me to expect that in an intimate relationship with another adult the loving, giving and supporting must go both ways.

I am so convinced that a reciprocal relationship is healthy that anything less than that is a clear warning to me that something is seriously wrong.

I don't feel a responsibility to make someone else happy.

I can watch a person I care about struggle with pain and be encouraging and supportive. But I don't feel it is my responsibility to relieve their pain.

I don't make excuses for unacceptable behaviors such as someone being selfish, rude, unkind, inconsiderate or controlling.

I have worked through all bitterness and unforgiveness toward anyone who has ever been hurtful or abusive toward me.

If I am drawn to a person, it is because I like him the way he was the day I met him. There is nothing about him that I need to work on helping him change.

Chapter Fifteen

How I Know I Haven't Changed Enough

The transformation of the human soul is a miracle that only the Lord can impart to us.

While we are in the midst of the process of Him helping us grow into a whole person, we need to be cautious about all our relationship decisions.

This is especially true if we have a history of choosing to get involved with people who mistreat us.

Until we have grown strong in what it means to walk in wholeness, we are still very vulnerable to making serious mistakes about people.

Some of the ways I can tell I will still be attracted to an unhealthy person...

I am still energized and motivated by feeling needed by another person. Consequently, I will attract needy people who will lean on me for their needs to be met.

I still like to take care of people to an extreme. I like to help people way too much. I tend to mother adults. Therefore I will easily become another adult's parent, caregiver, nurturer, therapist or counselor and I will attract people for a relationship who are looking for someone to take care of them.

I feel overwhelmed by the pressure of assuming responsibility for my own financial or emotional needs and I want someone to come along and rescue me from these pressures and take care of me. I am drawn to a relationship that appears to be a very good escape from these pressures. Consequently, I'm not ready for a healthy relationship because a healthy relationship is always between two people who take responsibility for their own needs and issues.

I feel sorry for people. I see adults who have been hurt as victims rather than as people who have choices about how they can respond to what has happened to them. As a result, I am extremely vulnerable to being manipulated into feeling sorry for a person. Consequently, I will be easily deceived into thinking that the sympathy I feel is love, when it is an extremely unhealthy counterfeit.

I want someone to feel sorry for me so I will repel a healthy person. Healthy people know better than to get drawn into feeling sorry for me.

I just ended an unhealthy relationship and I foolishly think that I am ready to launch right into another close relationship. As a result, I am setting myself up for walking into another mistake. Until I slow down and do some serious homework on why I have been stuck in a repeated cycle of getting close to unhealthy people, I will continue to repeat that same pattern. I will keep on gravitating to one person after another who is a serious mistake for my life.

I still dwell on the past. No healthy person is going to be attracted to someone who wants to think and talk about our hurts, betrayals or abuse in previous relationships. Therefore, until I put the past behind me, I'm not ready to attract a healthy person. There is also an alarming probability that until I change in this area I will attract other miserable people who will dwell on their own past hurts.

I still gravitate toward controlling people who want to run my life instead of being drawn toward people who respect who I am and the decisions I make.

I still have to be in a relationship to feel complete. I can't stand being alone, ever. To be alone means that I automatically feel lonely.

When I am in a relationship I still make excuses for their behaviors that are unacceptable, such as being unkind, inconsiderate, rude, selfish, stingy and oblivious to my feelings and needs.

I'm still too willing to suffer. I'm too willing to accept second best. I still don't say to myself when a relationship is painful…

> "This doesn't feel good.
>
> I deserve better.
>
> It isn't supposed to hurt to be in a relationship with someone who says they love me."

I am willing to pour my finances, time, help and love into someone who doesn't demonstrate an equal willingness to be there for me. I'm still willing to give and give and give and settle for the mere hope that if I give enough, maybe some day the other person will also give mutually toward me. Consequently selfish, demanding, emotionally unavailable people are drawn to me like a giant magnet.

I am too willing and too quick to accommodate, adapt or flex with what another person needs or wants. I have not as yet developed the skill to be honest about my true feelings and needs.

I haven't learned to put just as high a value on what I feel or need as I do on what another person feels or needs. As a result, I will attract people who are rigid, stubborn and selfish.

Out of fear of losing a relationship, I hesitate to be honest when I'm uncomfortable or if I disagree. This hesitation is an automatic recipe for disaster. It just about guarantees I will attract an unhealthy person. A whole, healthy person will not stick around once they realize that I'm not someone they can trust to be emotionally honest and up front with them. But unhealthy people will love my reluctance to speak my mind. My inability to be direct about my honest feelings allows the other person in the relationship to be demanding, abusive, selfish and controlling, all with a minimum amount of hassles from us. This is exactly the kind of person that abusive, selfish people are seriously attracted to.

Chapter Sixteen

I Am Worthy Of Being Loved

To become a whole person who can establish healthy relationships we must decide…

"I am worthy of being loved.

I am lovable because God tells me I am."

The Father assures us that our being this cherished by Him is exactly the way He feels about us…

"You are precious in My sight.
You are honored and I love you."
Isaiah 43:4 NASB

Because we are so precious to the Lord, we deserve to be treated with kindness, respect, tenderness and love. Never again can it be acceptable for anyone to be cruel to us.

To protect us from people who will mistreat us, the Father gives us this clear instruction…

"You are not to associate with anyone who
claims to be a Christian, yet is abusive.
Don't even eat with such people."
1 Corinthians 5:11 NLT

The revelation that we are worthy to be loved is basic to being a whole person. Therefore if we end up in one abusive relationship after another, we are not convinced that this is the truth. If we really believed it, we would never allow anyone to abuse us again.

The following incident reveals the defining moment in my life when I finally made this radically life-changing decision...

> During the last year of my second marriage, I sat in a chair across from Richard in our bedroom. He sat at a distance on the bed and leaned stiffly against the wall behind him. In icy silence he waited for me to explain to him why I was feeling terribly troubled.
>
> "I'm so unhappy in this marriage," I began as my voice quaked with emotion, "that I am struggling with thoughts about wanting to die."
>
> I paused and looked at Richard, hoping to see some indication that he cared about how much I was suffering. But he merely nodded his head to indicate he heard me. He was indifferent to my distress.
>
> "If I don't die," I continued as my body trembled with nervousness, "then I find myself wishing you would die so that I could be free. I don't know how much longer I can hurt in this marriage."
>
> He stared at me with no emotion whatsoever.
>
> I had invested fourteen years of my life trying to love this man and his coldness stung.
>
> He made no movement toward me to comfort me. He offered no response to my suicidal anguish.
>
> "After all these years I'm convinced you've never loved me," I continued in a strained, hurt voice.

"You are probably right. I probably never have," he replied with ugly disdain.

At that moment I made a proclamation.

"I am no longer willing to do all the loving and giving in any relationship," I said as I stood up.

"For the first time I really do believe I'm a loveable person and I'm worthy of being loved and cherished. I will no longer accept being treated with cruelty. This is the last time I will allow anyone to abuse me ever again."

I walked quietly out of the room and knew that no matter what price I had to pay, what I had just decided and boldly declared would change the course of my life.

In the months following that declaration, I struggled to understand what God expected of me.

Richard and I had spent most of our fourteen years in professional and pastoral counseling, but the problems continued unchanged. We had tried separation, but any improvement in our relationship disappeared shortly after we came back together. I had prayed for years for the marriage to be healed and it steadily deteriorated.

Most troubling of all, my heart ached over the damage my children had suffered from the years of constant abuse in our home.

The stress in the marriage had taken its toll on my physical health. I was sick more often than I was well.

Six months went by and a final incident erupted.

While I was in the hospital having major surgery, Richard's mother complained to him, "Ruth is the reason for all the problems in the family." She also called me and the minute I woke up from the anesthetic she told me this as well.

I was released from the hospital in less than twenty-four hours and as soon as I walked into the living room I asked Richard, "What did you say to your mother when she expressed this complaint about me?"

"I agreed with her," Richard replied with a smug look on his face. "It's true. Our family was doing great before you came along."

At that moment I recalled the conversation I had with him six months ago.

Here I was in pain once again because of his emotional betrayal. I was vulnerable physically due to the surgery and I felt extremely fragile emotionally. I needed my husband to protect me and treat me with kindness. Instead, Richard glared at me from a distance with cold indifference.

I calmly backed away from him and resolutely told him…

"That is the last time I will ever
allow you to abuse me again."

I walked out the door of our home that day and never returned.

Immediately the Father took me into His Papa God arms and sheltered me in His presence as I sought Him for direction for my new life. I knew that I had to be free of the constant pain that had battered me in this relationship. But I felt tremendous anguish about deciding to end another marriage.

I will never forget the tenderness the Father showed me as He revealed to me how He viewed this decision. Late one evening He ministered to my heart...

Picture how a loving father would feel toward you if you were his daughter. To him you are exceedingly precious.

Then one day you call him. You are sobbing hysterically as you explain to him...

"Dad, my husband is abusing me. He has been doing it for fourteen years. What do I do? I've tried so hard to make this marriage work. I've believed for so long that God could heal this relationship, but now I'm in so much pain that I want to die. And the children, Dad, they've been so hurt. They've suffered so much because of the abuse.

What do I do?"

"I don't want you to stay in this relationship and be destroyed," the father quickly responded. "You are too precious to me. You've tried your best.

Your mom and I both know that marriage is sacred and that ending a marriage is against God's Word. He has heard all your prayers for this relationship and He surely wants to bring healing into it. But neither you nor God have any control over the free will of another person who refuses to change. You can't make your husband change and God can't force him to change.

So be at peace that you have done all that you could possibly do to make this marriage succeed. Now it's time to come home. You have a safe place here to heal. Come and let your mother and I help you. You and the children have suffered long enough."

I cried and cried as I pondered this story. Then the Father interrupted my thoughts.

"Remember the Scripture…

> *'If a child asks her father for bread, he does not trick her with sawdust, does he? If she asks him for fish, he does not scare her with a live snake, does he? As bad as you are, you would not do that to your child. So do you think that I, Your Father, who conceived you in love, will do that to you? Matthew7 MESSAGE*

Yes, I hate divorce.

I hate all that it does to the sanctity of marriage because it is a union that is most sacred to Me.

I hate the splintering and shattering that divorce inflicts on innocent children.

But I also hate one of my precious children, who is the temple of My Spirit where My presence dwells, being maimed or crippled emotionally, mentally, sexually or physically by severe and relentless abuse from a spouse who won't listen to Me.

He won't let Me help him change.

And he has no intentions of stopping the abuse or changing the way he treats My precious child.

Has it not occurred to you that I, as your loving, caring Father, hate all of this as well?

If an earthly father wouldn't want his daughter to stay in a marriage in which abuse is destroying her and her children, why would you think I would require that of you?

Do you think I would love you less than an earthly father would love you? How could I ever say to you in My Word that you are 'precious, honored and I love you,' if I told you that I expect you and your children to accept being treated so cruelly and so abusively all the days of your life?

This would turn marriage into a horrible prison of pain for anyone who is married to someone who refuses to stop his abuse.

If I required that you stay in such a marriage, knowing all that I know, I would be a monster God. I would be an abusive Father. And not your Father who loves you and your children so very much."

Wearily I leaned back, rested my head against the chair and closed my eyes. I had never looked at my life in this way. I could hardly absorb the compassionate perspective that Papa God had just opened up to me. Then I gradually began to drink in His overwhelming kindness toward me and my children.

I took a deep breath and sighed audibly. Tension from a lifetime of trying to cope with being abused slowly drained out of me. From my first memory as a little girl, to be alive meant to hurt. Living with that mountain of pain was finally going to be over. From that day I gratefully began a new life because of my Abba Father's tender mercy and His compassionate forgiveness toward all my failures.

**All my life I lived in a land
where death cast its shadow.**

**But now I felt like my Abba Father
just made the sun come up.**
Matthew 4 MESSAGE/NLT

Chapter Seventeen

I Must Overcome Being Needy

To become a whole person who is attracted to relationships with whole, healthy people, we must often remind ourself that the less needy we are, then the more ready we are to establish a good relationship.

How I define needy...

We can't feel secure, happy or fulfilled unless we have a close relationship with the opposite sex. If we aren't in one of these relationships, we are miserable.

If we are alone, we are automatically lonely.

We are so insecure within ourself that we need constant affirmation. We are very dependent on other people to validate our worth as a person.

We lean heavily on other people to help us solve our problems rather than on the Lord.

To overcome being this needy was a major challenge for me. Even after I became a whole person, there were still moments when the decision to do whatever it takes to no longer look at life in this unhealthy way was very difficult for me.

I vividly recall one of those times...

I stood alone in the middle of my warmly decorated living room. It was quiet except for the steady tick of the clock on the wall nearby. I knelt in front of the couch and buried my face in my arms. I ached to have the arms of a man around me who would love me.

I longed to be held in the embrace of someone who would treat me with kindness.

"Please help me, Lord," I cried out. "Please help me."

I calmed down as soon as my Papa God reminded me of the Scripture He always spoke to me during my most difficult hours as a single woman. I had written it down and put it in an exquisite, heart-shaped frame on a prominent table. I looked up, glanced over at it as I wiped the tears from my eyes and read it…

**Delight yourself in Me
and I will give you the desires of your heart.**

Commit your way to Me.

Trust Me.

And I will do it.
Psalm 37:4-5 NASB

Once again I had to give all these intense longings and deeply felt needs to my Papa God. As I did, He took me by the hand and gently helped me to look at all of this through His eyes. And I could then comfort myself by saying to the Father…

"I am delighting in You.

Every day I passionately love You and every day I do long to be with You.

I have committed everything I am and everything I desire to You.

I do trust You with all my heart.

So Father, all over again I lay down this tremendous ache in my heart to be loved and I give it to You.

I release all of this to you once again. As I do, I thank You that I can find my way back to Your comforting peace. And I rest in the assurance of Your Word that You will give me the desires of my heart."

That was many years ago and God did keep His Word to me. He gave me the desires of my heart and He fulfilled my every longing.

Today I am experiencing the joy of a marriage between two healthy partners.

There are no control issues in this relationship and there is no abuse, ever.

I'm not my husband's mother and he's not my prince charming who rescued me from my troubles. He is a man who feels good about himself. So he doesn't need me to pump up his sagging self-worth. He also is not intimidated by my strengths or giftings.

We have a relationship based on mutual acceptance and encouragement toward each other.

Long before we met, we both had made our peace with the past and had put it behind us. We liked each other just the way we were and neither one of us would have pursued the relationship if we felt the other person wanted us to change.

We immediately had fun together and that has never changed. We can't recall a day when we haven't laughed about something.

I still chuckle when I recall the night Barry and I sat in his car and I realized that I was falling in love with him.

Here is how that moment unfolded...

Up to that point during the few times we had been together, Barry seemed to like me just the way I was and I was already letting my guard down. So we were quickly becoming friends. But there were certain things I promised myself I would say to any man before I allowed myself to get that close.

This was how I expressed my honesty to Barry that memorable evening...

> "I need to tell you some things about me," I began as I glanced over at him and then quickly looked straight ahead.
>
> Without pausing or even considering for a second how my directness was affecting him, I poured out my feelings about life, ministry and relationships.
>
> I explained to him my passion for life and for serving the Lord; my unwavering commitment to never again compromise what the Father had called me to do; my emotional independence; my determination to be the person God had created me to be; my refusal to change for any man ever again.

I even told him…

> *"I don't like to cook. So if you are looking for someone like that, well that isn't who I am at all."*

For the first time with a man, I didn't try to put my best foot forward and make a good impression. I actually did all I could to be so straightforward that if there was any possibility at all that this relationship was a mistake, it would be made extremely clear right away.

I earnestly wanted my blunt honesty to push Barry away from even wanting to know me, if he wasn't the right person for me to get involved with.

Consequently, when I finished speaking I was fully prepared for him to tell me…

> *"Ah, nice knowing you, but this is not what I'm looking for."*

So I was stunned when he turned toward me with a delightful twinkle in his blue eyes and a pleased grin spread warmly across his face.

"That's just the kind of person I'm looking for." he said without hesitation.

"Everything you've said is exactly how I feel too."

From that unforgettable night, a deep love immediately grew between us and the years we've been married have been the happiest for both of us.

We treasure each day God gives us to share together.

For me to live year after year with this kind, gentle man who so cherishes me is a taste of heaven here on earth.

His kindness toward my children has won their hearts. This has meant the world to me because they so needed to experience the faithful kindness of a special man just like Barry.

Now that I'm experiencing wholeness and peace on a daily basis, I can honestly say that ending my life long habit of choosing abusive, needy people to get involved with was the hardest thing I've ever had to overcome.

But the good news is that by the grace of God and through what I learned from His Word, I have succeeded in doing so.

My attraction to people who inflict pain is over.

All the heartache of the past is behind me. I'm a new person and the Father has given me a completely new life.

My damaged emotions that used to compel me to choose destructive relationships are healed.

The way I relate to people is drastically different from the years when I surrounded myself with unhealthy people. This transformation has been so complete that Barry has said to people…

> **"I'm amazed that Ruth has been through all that she has suffered in her past because in all the years we've been married, I haven't seen in her any indication that she has been through all of that. The Lord has made her that whole."**

God is "no respecter of persons" (Acts 10:34 NASB).

What He has done for me, He makes fully available to every person who cries out to Him.

He so longs to help and set us free that He pleads with us to hear His Father's heart if we are stuck in our pain.

And this is His heart…

"I will give you back your health.

I will heal all your wounds.

Just cry out to Me for help and I will restore your health.

I will not ignore your suffering.

I will not turn and walk away.

I promise you I will instantly listen to your cries for help.

And I will come to help you."
Jeremiah 30:17 NLT
Psalm 30:2, 22:24, 35:27 NLT

A closing personal message from the author...

Now that we have traveled together on this very personal journey, I earnestly pray that what you have read in *"A Trip To Freedom"* will minister an ongoing peace to you and a comforting hope. I also wish that its rich treasury of God's Word will keep on imparting courage and strength as you continue on with your search for wholeness and freedom. Thank you for letting me share my story with you. Now I encourage you to consider the **Two Sequels** to *"A Trip To Freedom."* I know they will help you tremendously as you press forward with all that the Father has planned for your life.

A Journey Toward Intimacy
The First Sequel to "A Trip To Freedom"

This book takes us beyond the place of healing.

It draws us into a deeper friendship with the Father that will help a person to keep on growing. It will also open up invaluable insights into what to do when life hurts in the present and as we walk into our future. The practical instructions in "A Trip To Freedom" will equip a person to experience a significant increase in healthy closeness in all the relationships that are the most dear to them.

My husband, Barry, and I are extremely transparent in this book so that our honesty can encourage and inspire each person who reads it in the intimacy they long for.

We Have A Dream

The Second Sequel to "A Trip To Freedom"

I wrote this book to challenge and inspire people to pursue their dream.

The Father does not heal us and give us the happiness we always longed for just for our personal enjoyment. He makes us whole and sets us free so that He can take everything we have ever been through and now use it to have a life-changing impact on other people. This impact is about stepping into our destiny. It is living our dream to make a difference. It is all about the Father using us in the powerful ways that were impossible when we were in so much pain.

In *"A Trip To Freedom"* we take an amazing walk toward finally being set free of the hurts of the past. But I guarantee that there is nothing more freeing or more rewarding than to finally have the courage to enter into what our life is all about.

The Father has glorious plans for each of us and He wants to help us understand how to fulfill those plans. Yet, multitudes of the Father's children live and die and never experience the destiny He has for them. They may even start out enthusiastically pursuing it. But eventually they are defeated. They give up because they don't understand what to do during the hard times to keep pressing on. It is in the pages of *"We Have A Dream"* that I share what I have learned is necessary to persevere in the purpose the Father has for our lives. I want to encourage you that the truths in this book will inspire you to *"Go for it!"* because you will understand how to rise up on wings like an eagle. In that rising up you will enter into an amazing freedom. You will have the courage to move forward with tenacious determination and unwavering faith, no matter what comes against the dream the Father has birthed in your heart.

My heartfelt wish is that you will be profoundly encouraged by reading *"We Have A Dream"* and at the end of it you can boldly declare, "Because the Sovereign Lord helps me, I will not be dismayed. Therefore I have set my face like flint, determined to do His will and I know that I will triumph." Isaiah 50:7 NLT

The author, Ruth Johnson, may be contacted at the address below.

To order:

A Trip To Freedom

The First Sequel to "A Trip To Freedom"
A Journey Toward Intimacy

The Second Sequel to "A Trip To Freedom"
We Have A Dream

Contact...

Lighthouse of Hope Ministries

PMB #365
914 164th Street SE #B-12
Mill Creek, Washington, U.S.A. 98012

(425) 775-3904

www.lighthouse-of-hope.org

ruth@lighthouse-of-hope.org
barry@lighthouse-of-hope.org